THE CHEROKEE NATION
AND THE TRAIL OF TEARS

THE PENGUIN LIBRARY OF AMERICAN INDIAN HISTORY

GENERAL EDITOR: COLIN G. CALLOWAY
Advisory Board: Brenda J. Child, Philip J. Deloria, Frederick E. Hoxie

THE
CHEROKEE NATION
AND
THE TRAIL OF TEARS

THEDA PERDUE AND
MICHAEL D. GREEN

THE PENGUIN LIBRARY
OF AMERICAN INDIAN HISTORY

VIKING

VIKING
Published by the Penguin Group
Penguin Group (USA) Inc., 375 Hudson Street, New York, New York 10014,
U.S.A.   ·   Penguin Group (Canada), 90 Eglinton Avenue East, Suite 700, Toronto,
Ontario, Canada M4P 2Y3 (a division of Pearson Penguin Canada Inc.)   ·   Penguin
Books Ltd, 80 Strand, London WC2R 0RL, England   ·   Penguin Ireland, 25 St
Stephen's Green, Dublin 2, Ireland (a division of Penguin Books Ltd)   ·   Penguin
Books Australia Ltd, 250 Camberwell Road, Camberwell, Victoria 3124, Australia
(a division of Pearson Australia Group Pty Ltd)   ·   Penguin Books India Pvt Ltd,
11 Community Centre, Panchsheel Park, New Delhi - 110 017, India   ·   Penguin
Group (NZ), 67 Apollo Drive, Rosedale, North Shore 0745, Auckland,
New Zealand (a division of Pearson New Zealand Ltd)   ·   Penguin Books (South
Africa) (Pty) Ltd, 24 Sturdee Avenue, Rosebank, Johannesburg 2196, South Africa

Penguin Books Ltd, Registered Offices: 80 Strand, London WC2R 0RL, England

First published in 2007 by Viking Penguin, a member of Penguin Group (USA) Inc.

ISBN-13: 978-0-670-03150-4

Printed in the United States of America
Set in Granjon
Designed by Katy Riegel

For Mary Young and Ray Fogelson

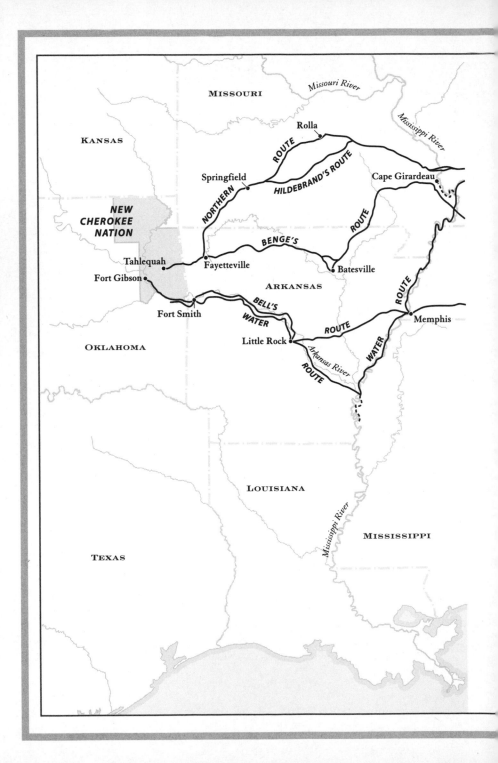

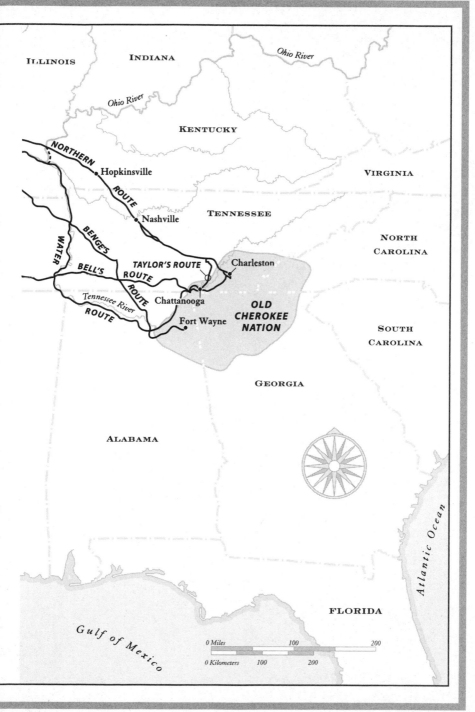

ILLINOIS

INDIANA

Ohio River

Ohio River

KENTUCKY

NORTHERN ROUTE

• Hopkinsville

VIRGINIA

Nashville

TENNESSEE

NORTH
CAROLINA

BENGE'S

WATER

BELL'S ROUTE

TAYLOR'S ROUTE

Charleston

Tennessee River ROUTE

Chattanooga

OLD
CHEROKEE
NATION

Fort Wayne

SOUTH
CAROLINA

GEORGIA

ALABAMA

FLORIDA

Atlantic Ocean

Gulf of Mexico

0 Miles   100   200

0 Kilometers   100   200

© 2007 Jeffrey L. Ward

CONTENTS

Contents

INTRODUCTION

ALL CHEROKEES ONCE lived in the southern Appalachians. In the eighteenth century, they claimed hunting grounds
that extended into Kentucky, but they clustered their villages
and agricultural fields in the valleys of upcountry South Carolina, western North Carolina, east Tennessee, north Georgia, and northeastern Alabama. They spoke four mutually
intelligible dialects of an Iroquoian language. A common
culture and bonds of kinship held their far-flung villages together and made them a people. Today, most Cherokees do
not live in the Southeast; they live in eastern Oklahoma with
only a small remnant remaining in the mountains of western
North Carolina. The United States recognizes three tribes—
the Cherokee Nation and United Keetoowah Band in Oklahoma and the Eastern Band of Cherokees in North Carolina.
The division of the Cherokees was not by choice. In the early

nineteenth century, the United States forced the Cherokee Nation to surrender its homeland and relocate west of the Mississippi. That event, known as the Trail of Tears, is the subject of this book.

The term "Trail of Tears," a rough translation of the Cherokee *nunna dual tsuny*, describes the trek of heartbroken people to their new homes in the West. The term captures the essence of the removal experience, but it also conveys the impression that removal was a uniquely Cherokee experience. Although that was not the case, there are reasons why scholars have so frequently told the story of Indian removal in Cherokee terms. One is that the debate over removal policy that occurred in the press, various public settings, and Congress focused on the Cherokees. The laws, treaties, and historical examples cited as the discussions progressed always related to the Cherokees. To many, the Cherokees demonstrated that Indians could change and that someday they could be integrated into American society. Furthermore, the Cherokee leaders during the removal crisis of the 1820s and 1830s were uniquely well educated and extraordinarily articulate in both spoken and written English. In countless public speeches and written statements, they produced a trove of documents that dwarfs the records of other Native nations. They were also masters of public relations. Their policy was to make certain that no one could forget them. The result is that the Cherokees have become the Indians whose name everyone knows, and the history of their suffering has come to represent the injustice that has characterized much of the relations between the United States and Native Americans. Only about 10 percent of the eastern Indians who traveled trails of tears to the place now called Oklahoma were Cherokees, however, and each of the dozens of relocated tribes has its own unique and important history. The history of the removal of the Cherokees can never substitute for the histories of the others, but it can exemplify a larger history that no one should forget.

The period in which Indian removal unfolded was one of contradictions. It was hailed by an earlier generation of historians as a period of expanding democratic institutions, but more recent scholars have pointed to the limitations on that democracy. In the early nineteenth century, states largely abolished property restrictions on voting and made it possible for all adult white men to exercise the franchise. At the same time, legislatures further limited the rights of women and free African Americans, and southern states enacted far more stringent slave codes. Legislation increased the number of offices filled by election, but the spoils system enabled the victors in elections to reward their political cronies with positions, contracts, and other perquisites of power. The wave of revivalism that began at the turn of the century brought more Americans into churches, but it created a split between those who believed in the perfectibility of society and those who focused on individual salvation. Southerners, in particular, tended to worry about their own souls and suspect those who dwelled on social ills. A market revolution both tied rural folk to national issues and left many of them in an economic backwater. The West was the land of promise to thousands of Americans, but its settlement by citizens of the United States spelled disaster for the Native peoples who already lived there. No one better understood the contradictions of this age of democracy than the Cherokees, who adopted many of its institutions only to suffer from the tyranny of the majority and who rejected whatever opportunities the West offered only to be forced there against their will.

The Trail of Tears is, without question, a Cherokee tragedy and an Indian tragedy, but it is also an American tragedy. When essayist Sarah Vowell retraced the Trail of Tears over which her Cherokee ancestors had traveled, she thought about Chief John Ross, who fought removal in Congress and before the United States Supreme Court: "He believed in the liberties the Declaration of Independence promises, and the civil rights the Constitution ensures. And when the U.S. betrayed not only the Cherokees but its own creed I would guess that John Ross was not only angry, not only outraged, not only confused, I would guess that John Ross was a little brokenhearted. Because that's how I feel. I've been experiencing the Trail of Tears not as a Cherokee, but as an American."[1] Vowell is right. Cherokees believed in the promise of democracy and the justice of the United States, and their disappointment is a legacy that all Americans share.

THE CHEROKEE NATION
AND THE TRAIL OF TEARS

1

THE LAND AND THE PEOPLE

IN THE BEGINNING there was no land, just water and sky. The animals lived above the solid rock vault that formed the sky, but they were very crowded. The little water beetle, beaver's grandchild, volunteered to see what was below the water. The little beetle found soft mud and brought it to the surface where it began to grow and form the island that became the earth. But the earth had to dry and become firm before the animals could make their homes there. The Great Buzzard went down to see if it was ready, and he flew low over the land. By the time he reached the Cherokee country, he was tired and his wings struck the ground making valleys and mountains. When the animals finally descended to their new home, it was dark. Therefore they placed the sun on a track to cross the island every day from east to west before slipping under the vault of the sky, and their conjurors, or priests, raised it seven times until it was high enough to provide light and warmth without burning the earth's new inhabitants. This land of mountains and valleys and gentle sun was the home of the Cherokees. The first human beings to live in this land, a brother and a sister, came after the plants and animals. When the brother struck his sister with a fish, which the Cherokees associate with fertility, she began to give birth to a child every seven days until there were so many people, they feared, that the world could not hold them all. Consequently women began to bear no more than one child a year, and the Cherokees' world was safe, at least until the Europeans came.[1]

When Europeans first arrived in 1540, the Cherokees still lived in the mountains that the newcomers called the Appalachians after an unrelated tribe, the Apalachees, who lived to the south. Like the Cherokees, the Europeans believed that their ancestors, Adam and Eve, had lived in a paradise created for them, but their god had expelled them from the Garden of Eden for a flaw with which Cherokees would become all too familiar—they could not be content with what they had. The apple that Eve offered Adam promised more, and when Adam sank his teeth into it, they and their descendants got far more than they had bargained for—a life of toil, death, the pain of childbirth. Cast out of the Garden of Eden, they became wanderers, always seeking more.

The early Cherokees were not without their own problems. Like Adam and Eve, the first couple, Kana'tĭ and Selu, lived in a land of abundant resources. Kana'tĭ provided his family with game from a cave that he covered with a large rock, and Selu got corn and beans by rubbing her stomach and armpits in the storehouse. When their son and Wild Boy, a mysterious child who had emerged from the river, discovered the secret of the game, they tried to imitate Kana'tĭ, but, lacking his skill, they let all the animals escape so that afterward Cherokees had to hunt for game. They killed Selu because they believed that she was a witch. Before she died, Selu instructed them to clear a circle and drag her body around it seven times, but they only prepared seven small patches and dragged her body around them twice. This is why corn does not grow everywhere and Cherokees hoe the crop twice. Other Cherokees came from distant places to get corn to plant for their villages. The boys gave them seven grains and told them to plant the kernels each evening of their seven-day journey. Following instructions, they stayed awake all night, and each morning they had seven ripe ears to take home to their people. But on the seventh night, they fell asleep, and ever since, Cherokees have had to tend their crops for half the year instead of just one night. Instead of being forced from their homeland like Adam and Eve, the Cherokees learned how to live in it.

The lessons of how to live in the world were not always easy ones. In the old days, plants, animals, and people had lived together peacefully, but people increased so rapidly that they began to crowd the animals. Even worse, humans invented weapons that they used to kill the larger animals, and they trampled the smaller animals underfoot without giving any thought to the lives they were taking. The animals decided to make war on humans, but, when the bears tried to use the bows and arrows they had constructed, their claws hung on the bowstring. They gave up, leaving the deaths of their kin unpunished. The deer, however, decided to use their spiritual power and send rheumatism to afflict hunters who killed them without asking pardon of the deer's spirit. Other species followed the example of the deer and devised diseases to punish people who did not respect their right to inhabit the earth along with human beings. The plants overheard the animals and decided to help people by providing medicine to counteract disease. In this way, plants balanced animals. Cherokees began to perform rituals to avoid the illnesses brought by animal spirits and to learn from the spirits of plants how to cure sickness. Although they were rife with conflict, the creation stories of the Cherokees emphasized the importance of respect for other living things, not dominion over them.[2]

Spiritual forces shaped the world in which the Cherokees lived, and knowledge, ceremonies, and rules enabled them to call on those forces when they needed to do so. The Cherokees associated spiritual power not only with plants and animals but also with rivers, mountains, caves, and other land forms. These features served as mnemonic devices to remind them of the beginning of the world, the spiritual forces that inhabited it, and their responsibilities to it. Unlike the Garden of Eden, which had disappeared into the mists of time, the Cherokees could point to the mountains created by the Great Buzzard and to one particular mountain, Kuwâ' hĭ, or Clingmans Dome, where the bears met in council to plot their revenge on humans. Land forms also called to mind important life lessons. For example, Cherokees knew that Spear-finger, a monster who took the shape of an old woman who had a stone finger that she used to kill people, had frequented the headwaters of the Nantahala River and had sought victims near villages in the valley below Chilhowee Mountain. When they saw these places, they remembered the trap that villagers had set for Spear-finger and the little chickadee that showed the warriors the location of Spear-finger's heart by alighting on her hand. If the people had not cooperated to dig a pit across the trail, conceal it with brush, and build a campfire to attract the monster to what she thought would be victims, the warriors would not have had an opportunity to attack her. If the warriors had not recognized that other creatures, even little chickadees, knew things that they did not know, they would not have aimed their arrows at Spear-finger's clenched fist. The lessons taught by the Cherokee landscape were central, not only to accounts of the distant past, but to the ways they lived their lives every day.[3]

The fundamental religious principles of the Cherokees were not recorded in a hefty tome and preached in a towering cathedral, but written on the land and lived in interaction with it. Cherokees knew that this was the land meant for them, and their cosmology located them in the center. The cardinal points converged in the Cherokees' homeland, and they associated each direction with certain colors and characteristics.

The North (blue) represented trouble and defeat, the South (white) peace and happiness, the East (red) success and victory, the West (black) death. Conjurors invoked the directions and the colors associated with them in their sacred formulas—the East or the South to help their clients and the North or the West to destroy their enemies—and rituals usually took place in relation to the cardinal points.[4]

The Cherokees' attachment to their homeland rested on far more than cosmology and the primordial past. "The land was given to us by the Great Spirit above as our common right," a council of Cherokee women asserted in 1818, "to raise our children upon and to make support for our rising generations."[5] Abandoning their homeland at the world's center, and moving west, the direction associated with death, was unthinkable. The land and its resources were theirs to use, as long as they showed proper respect, and they depended on it for their subsistence. Because of their dependence on the land, the Cherokees knew their environment intimately.

Game filled the forests, and the Cherokees, who had no domesticated animals, depended on it. The white-tailed deer was the most important game animal, followed by the bear. Cherokee men knew the habits and characteristics of their prey, so they hunted deer at dawn and dusk as the animals browsed on tender shrubs along the forest edge, and they sought bears in caves or hollow trees. They understood the spawning and feeding habits of fish, and they constructed stone weirs, still visible today in the rivers of western North Carolina, so that they could net, trap, shoot, or poison their catch more easily. They hunted wild turkeys and other fowl as well as small mammals, such as squirrels and groundhogs, with traps and blowguns made from a native bamboo called river cane. Killing any animals (except bears, who had failed in their attempt at vengeance on humans) required special ceremonies, prayers, and songs. As a further show of respect, Cherokees used virtually all of the mammals, fish, and fowl that they killed. They ate the meat, tanned the hides, made tools of the bones and antlers, turned sinews into thread, and employed claws, teeth, and feathers as ceremonial items. Little went to waste.

The forests of the Cherokee homelands provided a far richer subsistence than just game. Giant poplar trees became dugout canoes. Large trees supported the roofs of Cherokee houses while woven saplings plastered with mud formed the walls. Women wove mats and baskets for their houses from river cane, which they dyed with a variety of substances such as bloodroot and walnuts. They coiled clay dug from river banks into pots, which they fired in their hearths. Women also gathered a host of wild foods—onions, mushrooms, greens, nuts, berries, grapes, and the roots, leaves, and seeds of scores of other plants. Cherokees used salt from springs and licks to preserve meat and flint and chert from outcroppings to make points and blades. They also claimed a pharmacopoeia of over eight hundred herbs. Nature's bounty, however, was not as easily accessible as this recounting suggests: Cherokees had learned over centuries how to use this abundance.[6]

Cherokees were conscious of being part of the natural world, and they did their best to conserve it. The rituals associated with hunting required that men kill game, especially deer, only if they truly needed it. Similarly, Cherokees protected the flora of the homeland. In collecting ginseng, an important medicine, collectors passed the first three plants they found in the forest and took only the fourth one. As recently as the spring of 2005, a letter to the *Cherokee One Feather*, the newspaper of the Eastern Band of Cherokee Indians, complained that white people were pulling up ramps, or wild onions, by the roots rather than cutting them off, a practice that ensured the plant's survival.

Awareness and conservation, however, do not mean that Cherokees did not alter their environment: They did. They built villages on sites that they had cleared from the forest, and in the fall they burned the underbrush in the woods surrounding their villages to improve visibility, eliminate undesirable scrub oaks, and encourage forage for deer. Through constant use they created trails that linked villages and extended beyond the area of settlement to neighboring tribes and hunting grounds. And above all, the Cherokees opened fields where they grew large crops of corn, beans, squash, and sunflowers.

Except for the earthen mounds built by their Mississippian progenitors, enormous fields were the most visually impressive feature of southeastern Indian life. Farming in the Southeast probably began about 3000 B.C.E. when women, who were the gatherers of wild foods, began to cultivate some of the plants that they collected. Soon they began to grow squash. By C.E. 300, they were planting corn, and about

C.E. 1000, beans appeared on the scene. Cherokees were a part of this agricultural revolution in the Southeast. Although they speak an Iroquoian language that is very different from the Muskogean and Siouan languages spoken by most of their neighbors in the Southeast, linguists think that the Cherokees split off from northern Iroquois people at least thirty-five hundred years ago. By the time Europeans arrived, Cherokees had been in the region for a very long time and participated fully in the agricultural economy that had given rise to the Mississippian cultural tradition. This culture emerged about C.E. 800 in the Mississippi valley and by 1000 it had reached the ancestors of the Cherokees. The construction of flat-top mounds, hierarchical political systems called chiefdoms, and an elaborate religious life characterized Mississippian societies. Although Cherokees no longer built mounds when Europeans arrived, their villages often included these structures, their religious beliefs had roots in Mississippian culture, and their extensive fields connected them to the Mississippian past.[7]

In the Cherokees' gendered division of labor, women did most of the farming. Men helped clear the land and plant the crops, and they joined in the harvest, but primary responsibility for cultivation rested with women. Cherokees owned their land in common, and individuals had the right to clear and use land as long they did not infringe on their neighbors. Households divided the large fields that surrounded villages into separate sections, but women worked together, moving from one household's section to another's hoeing their crops.

[9]

Each family usually also maintained a small kitchen garden near its dwelling. Cherokee families were matrilocal, that is, they lived in the household of the mother, not the father, and descent was matrilineal—kin ties passed through women, not men. Houses and fields, therefore, descended from mothers to daughters. Cherokees also received their clan affiliation from their mothers.[8]

Cherokees had seven clans, or large extended families, that traced their ancestry back to a common, mythical ancestor. Clan members were scattered throughout Cherokee villages, which reportedly numbered sixty-four in the mid-eighteenth century, and served to unite Cherokees. Until the late 1700s, Cherokees do not seem to have had a centralized government. Clans provided protection by seeking restitution and retribution for wrongs done to their members, and corporate decisions were made at the clan or town level. This political decentralization, however, does not mean that Cherokees did not think of themselves as a people—they did—but that identity rested on the ties of kinship, language, and shared beliefs, all of which connected them to their homeland.

The Cherokees inscribed their identity on the landscape. The land forms and rivers in the Cherokees' homeland had names that they had given them. Since Cherokees spoke a language distinct from that of their neighbors, the names of these land forms undeniably marked the country as Cherokee. Cherokee names for many of these places have persisted, and even for those Europeans renamed, some Cherokees still know them by their original designations. The land expressed

Cherokee identity in other ways. The specific sections of fields and the clusters of buildings that composed homesteads bespoke the kin ties that shaped Cherokee life. Other markers commemorated kin, especially those whose blood soaked the soil in wars with Europeans and other Indian tribes. In western North Carolina, for example, a rock pyramid that memorialized women and children murdered by an Iroquois war party in the late eighteenth century endured until the late twentieth century because Cherokees continued to add a stone when they passed it.

The first Europeans to arrive in the Cherokee homeland were members of the Hernando de Soto expedition of 1539–43, followed by the Juan Pardo expedition in 1566–68.[9] For the next century, Cherokees had little contact with Europeans, but they nevertheless felt their effect. Like other Native Americans, the Cherokees had little immunity to European diseases, and epidemics that Europeans sparked decimated their population. The first documented epidemic was in 1697, although earlier epidemics may well have struck, and wave after wave of disease pummeled the Cherokees. From a pre-epidemic population of approximately 30,000 to 35,000, the number of Cherokees had dropped to 11,210 people in 1715 and perhaps less than 7,000 by the mid-1760s. Although European imperial wars and conflicts with Indian neighbors took many lives, disease was the major factor in depopulation. Population decline sent a powerful message to Europeans— the Cherokees were in the process of disappearing and, consequently, they needed far less land than they once had.[10]

Europeans generally recognized that Indians had a right to the land. Their respect for that right varied widely, and the right of discovery, which Europeans claimed, often took precedence over any rights accorded Indian people. Native Americans, Europeans believed, had deficiencies that compromised their title. First of all, they were not Christian, a major concern of the Spanish and later the French, both of whom sponsored widespread missionary efforts. Second, they were "uncivilized," an amorphous disability that included their lack of proper clothing and houses as well as their "heathen" rituals, government, military tactics, families, and economies. By the eighteenth century, the English, in particular, had come to rank human societies by their cultural complexity, which they tended to define in economic terms. They regarded hunting and gathering as the least complex economic basis for society, followed by livestock herding, farming, and finally their own mixed economies of commerce, manufacturing, and agriculture as the most complex. People who were "heathen" and "uncivilized" had no absolute title to their land. Instead, they had the right of occupancy, and when they vacated the land, it became the property of the discoverer. The discoverer who had the strongest claim to the Cherokees' homeland was England.

From the early English settlements along the Atlantic coast, the Cherokee country was remote and rugged, but it promised a lucrative trade in deerskins and other pelts for which there was considerable demand in Europe. By the end of the seventeenth century, traders were beginning to make their way to Cherokee villages, and within a few years English traders had taken up residence in most Cherokee communities. They stocked a range of European manufactured goods including brass kettles, metal hatchets and hoes, scissors and knives, textiles, and trinkets. In addition, they sold guns and ammunition, which the Cherokees needed to protect themselves from their enemies, also armed by the English, who sought war captives to sell as slaves to work on English plantations alongside African Americans. Some Cherokees fell victim to slave-raiders; others captured and sold slaves themselves.[11]

Cherokees traded beeswax and river cane baskets as well as slaves, but the mainstay of commerce with the English was deerskins, which Europeans used to make a variety of leather goods including gloves and knee breeches. The centrality of deerskins to the early relationship between the English and the Cherokees gave the English a rather skewed impression of the Cherokee economy. Ignoring the Cherokees' reliance on agriculture, the English depicted them primarily as hunters. Some went so far as to suggest that the land was so rich that corn and beans practically sprouted on their own and required little labor. Thomas Jefferson, for example, wrote in the 1780s that "all the nations of Indians in North America lived in the hunter state and depended for subsistence on hunting, fishing, and the spontaneous fruits of the earth," adding as an afterthought that women planted corn.[12] The role of women as farmers contributed to the perception that farming played a secondary role in the Cherokee economy: If it had been truly important, Englishmen reasoned, the Indians surely would not have put women in charge. The view that Indians were hunters and gatherers rather than farmers gained considerable currency in North America even as Englishmen adopted both Indian crops—corn, beans, and squash—and agricultural techniques, such as hilling rather than broadcasting seeds.

Colonization coincided with transformations in English agriculture and land tenure. In the Middle Ages, which were coming to a close just as England embarked on overseas empire-building, the English had employed an open field system in which peasants cultivated designated strips in large fields owned by their landlords. They grazed their livestock on common land, which also provided firewood and other resources. During the period of colonization, however, English landowners were in the process of consolidating grazing land for sheep production, a move that dislocated many peasants and restricted the economic production of others. Indian land holding and use were remarkably similar to the system of open fields and common lands that the English were abandoning as inefficient. By comparison to England, with its displaced peasants crowding into cities, North America, which had been substantially depopulated, seemed empty as well as underused. Englishmen believed that Indian land fell far short of its potential productivity. The economic opportunism that led to enclosure also prompted small landowners, often called yeoman farmers, to acquire land from large landowners who had overextended themselves and to seek their fortunes in the New World. This acquisitiveness meant that most Englishmen whom the Cherokees encountered considered Indian land and resources to be new opportunities to enrich themselves. Whatever designs the English had on Indian land, however, by the eighteenth century they recognized Indian tribal sovereignty in two ways: They negotiated treaties with them and they prohibited encroachment by colonists on Indian land.

Beginning perhaps as early as 1684 the English negotiated treaties with the Cherokees. Treaties implied sovereignty, that is, the right of a people to govern themselves. The early treaties the Cherokees signed with the English governed the relationship between the two people by establishing alliances and setting the prices of the goods they traded. In 1730 seven Cherokee headmen traveled to London where they entered into a treaty in which they acknowledged English sovereignty. The Cherokees agreed to refrain from trade, alliances, or friendship with other European powers and to deliver up African-American slaves who sought refuge among them. The Cherokees understood alliances, but in their decentralized political system, such agreements bound only the individuals who made them, not the entire people. The English, on the other hand, understood treaties to be binding and to subordinate the Cherokees to their imperial power.

Alliances with the Cherokees were useful to the English in a number of imperial conflicts. Over two hundred Cherokees, for example, joined other Indians and the Carolina militia to defeat the Tuscaroras in 1711–13. In the 1750s the English secured permission to build forts in the Cherokee country to prevent the French from gaining a foothold, and in 1756 about a hundred Cherokees joined a Virginia expedition against the French-allied Shawnee in the Ohio River valley. On their way home, the warriors skirted the Virginia frontier where frontiersmen killed a number of them, setting off a chain of events that included the murder of Cherokee hostages by the English, the invasion and defeat of an English army, and the Cherokee capture of the English fort west of the mountains. The war ended in 1760 with an English invasion of the Cherokees' homeland and the destruction of Cherokee towns, cornfields, and granaries.[13]

The Cherokee War marked the beginning of a political transformation. The English had long pretended that a national government existed among the Cherokees and sought to make treaties signed by a few binding on all, but in reality, towns were independent and individuals often pursued courses that no government sanctioned. A nascent national council may have existed before the war, but in the years following Cherokee defeat, warriors began to take a more active role in uniting Cherokee towns and controlling any actions by individuals that might jeopardize the safety of the entire tribe.[14] By the end of the century, they had been joined by others whose skills were needed, especially those Cherokees who were literate in English. These political changes culminated nearly seven decades after the Cherokee War in the creation of the Cherokee constitutional republic that resisted removal.

The Cherokee War was one phase of a broader conflagration, the Seven Years War, also called the French and Indian War, that concluded with the British as the most powerful European empire in North America. But the war had strained British resources, and the Crown recognized that friction between colonists and Indians had contributed to its cause and had prompted most Indians to side with the French. Consequently, the king issued the Proclamation of 1763 that prohibited English settlement west of the Appalachians, a line that ran through Cherokee country. The Proclamation of 1763 formalized a demographic that already had emerged in the English colonies—Indians and English did not live together. Even in New England where Indians had converted to Christianity and established "praying towns," Native communities existed apart from English ones. There was some intermarriage, but usually the non-Indian spouse and the children became a part of Indian society rather than vice versa. Although the English gave lip service to the notion of assimilation, the creation of an Indian country suggested that few believed it to be an attainable goal. A separate and distinct Indian country, however, also tacitly recognized the proprietary rights of Indian tribes. Treaties were the documents by which the English acquired those proprietary rights.

Between 1721 and 1777, the Cherokees entered into nine agreements, in which they ceded approximately half of their land to the English.[15] Most of this land was hunting grounds, which Cherokees often shared with other tribes, or land, like that in upcountry South Carolina, onto which English colonists encroached. With one exception, the English regarded these treaties as agreements between governments, and even Richard Henderson's private purchase of 1775 ended up being claimed by North Carolina and Virginia. The precedent that the English established for the United States, therefore, was that individuals could not purchase Indian land; only the government could. That means that a backcountry farmer in South Carolina could not legally buy Cherokee land; only the agents of the Crown (and that included colonial officials) could do so. Colonists chafed at this restriction, especially after the Proclamation of 1763. Their resentment fanned the fires of revolution.

The Proclamation was of little practical benefit to the Cherokees. Colonial officials continued to demand land cessions, which the Cherokees resisted as best they could, but often the tract in question already had been overrun by colonists. Consequently, Cherokee headmen signed treaties and ceded land. But colonists did not confine their expansion to ceded territory. They illegally occupied Cherokee land and refused to move. When the American Revolution began, most Cherokees sided with the king, who had issued the Proclamation, rather than the colonists, who violated it with impunity. Once again the Cherokees became victims of invasion and destruction. One militiaman reported that his comrades had killed and scalped sixteen warriors and fired on a fleeing woman whom they wounded, interrogated, and then killed "to put her out of her pain." His company was ordered "to destroy, cut down, and burn all the vegetables belonging to our heathen enemies." Another company took two women and a boy captive and threatened to kill and scalp them unless the officers permitted them to sell the captives as slaves. They brought twelve hundred dollars.[16] Although a group of Cherokees known as Chickamaugas continued to fight until 1794, most Cherokees laid down their weapons in 1781.

The American invasions devastated the Cherokee homeland, and a series of cessions had reduced their land base dramatically, but the heart of the Cherokee country remained theirs. In the valleys of the southern Appalachians, the Cherokees resolved to rebuild their towns, replant their fields and orchards, and rekindle the strong sense of identity that linked them to their homeland. When they did begin to rebuild, they exhibited all the ingenuity of the little water beetle, the Great Buzzard, and their own ancestors in transforming their country and their people to meet new challenges.

2

"CIVILIZING" THE CHEROKEES

"I WILL TELL YOU about the Cherokees. I think they improve," a young Cherokee girl wrote a New England clergyman in 1828. "They have a printing press and print a paper which is called the Cherokee Phoenix. They come to meeting on Sabbath days. They wear clothes which they made themselves. Some though rude, have shoes and stockings. They keep horses, cows, sheep, and swine. Some have oxen. They cultivate fields. . . . I hope this nation will soon become civilized and enlightened." The Cherokee Nation she described represented the fulfillment of one goal of the first United States Indian policy, and the hope she expressed for the future echoed the words of policymakers over a quarter century before.[1] Henry Knox was the primary architect of the "civilization" policy, the program that had enabled the cultural transformation of the Cherokees that Sally Reese described so proudly. Secretary of war in the governments of both the Articles of Confederation and the first administration of President George Washington, his main concern was the security of the new United States. Congress had defined the Indian tribes as security problems and charged the War Department with the management of relations with them. In the early years of independence, conducting Indian affairs was the overriding national security challenge. Knox believed that "civilizing" the Indians would both bring and perpetuate peace with them.

The Treaty of Paris of 1783 recognized the independence of the United States and defined the boundaries of the new nation to include all the territory east of the Mississippi River between the Great Lakes and Spanish Florida. Indians were not present, nor were their interests represented, at the talks in Paris and thus played no role in shaping the treaty. The United States won the claims of sovereignty over its territory that England had asserted under the right of conquest. The United States also acquired from England a history of interactions with Indian tribes. England and the colonies had often negotiated treaties with Native nations that established peace, regulated trade, and purchased land. At least since the Proclamation of 1763, England had recognized the rights of tribes to their lands and appointed special officials to buy and pay for those rights. These relations were often tense, and the Cherokees, along with many other tribes, frequently found themselves pressured into selling lands they would have preferred to keep, but the system of purchase by treaty was a well-established one that everyone understood, and the Indians, at least, expected to continue.

Some states owned enormous tracts of land that their colonial charters granted them. To appease states that did not have western territory, the United States began to acquire the lands of those that did. In 1784, Virginia granted to the United States its claim to the region west of the Appalachian Mountains and north of the Ohio River, thereby placing it under the authority of Congress. South of the Ohio River, Virginia retained present Kentucky, North Carolina claimed present Tennessee, and Georgia held present Alabama and Mississippi. Large numbers of Indians, including Cherokees, lived on these lands that the states were reluctant to surrender. According to the Articles of Confederation, under which the United States was governed until 1789, the states held the right to deal with the tribes within their borders while Congress had the responsibility for conducting relations with Indians who lived beyond the states. Both Congress and the states were eager to make the lands of western tribes available to American citizens, but none had the money to pay Indians for land. Believing that the recent victory over England made them invincible, they simultaneously developed Indian policies that ignored tribal land rights and dictated treaties that took without payment huge tracts of land. The treaties defined the tribes as defeated enemies, providing a justification of this policy. The United States insisted that the right of conquest doctrine, which had required England to surrender its claims to the United States, also applied to the tribes. By this reasoning, the tribes had no rights to the land and could expect to receive no compensation for the country they had to relinquish.

The first treaty the Cherokees concluded with the United States after the Revolution, the 1785 Treaty of Hopewell, did not reflect this confiscatory policy. Embroiled in conflict in the Ohio valley with Indians fighting to defend themselves from its confiscation policy, Congress feared that similar demands on southern tribes would widen the war. Instead, the United States recognized Cherokee land rights and agreed to respect them. But Georgia and North Carolina confiscated large tracts from the Nation, and the breakaway state of Franklin, organized by secessionist Carolinians in present Tennessee, confiscated more. The tribes refused to tolerate such treatment. Except for the Cherokees, most had not been invaded during the Revolution by American armies, and even among the Cherokees, many warriors had sided with the colonists. None considered themselves to have been defeated, and they absolutely rejected the right-of-conquest pretensions of Congress and the states. They insisted that future relations must be conducted according to the well-established procedures: They must be treated with the respect due to sovereign nations, their legitimate claims to their territories must be recognized, and any arrangements to surrender lands must be accomplished through duly negotiated treaties with designated tribal leaders and paid for by money and goods.

This was the mess Henry Knox found waiting for him when he assumed office in 1785. The tribes from Ohio to

Georgia defended their rights by warfare, the frontier was aflame, and the secretary of war could not protect the lives and property of American citizens. He had neither an army nor the money to get one. He quickly concluded that the main cause of the trouble was the aggressive, confiscatory Indian policies of Congress and the states that encouraged their citizens to invade Indian country, take tribal land, kill Indians who got in their way, and then demand protection when the Indians acted to defend themselves and their homeland. Knox believed that the Indians were correct in their insistence that Americans must respect their sovereignty, recognize their territorial rights, and negotiate and pay for the land they wished to acquire. He also knew that the tribes would not surrender their lands without a long and bloody fight, which the United States could afford neither financially nor morally. Knox thought such a war would contravene the principles of justice, honor, and humanity for which he had fought in the Revolutionary War. Such a war would result in the destruction of the Indians, he believed, and give the United States a reputation for rapacity and dishonor that future historians would condemn.

The only way to achieve peace was to develop an Indian policy that the Indians would accept and that would ultimately achieve the aims of the states. That is why "civilization" was at the center of Knox's thinking. Like other educated men of the Revolutionary era, Knox was an adherent of the Enlightenment. This intellectual movement began in Europe and spread to North America in the eighteenth century. Its ideas formed the basis of the Declaration of Independence, whose words "all men are created equal" were a basic tenet. Knox and his colleagues recognized differences in human beings, but they also believed that, with opportunity and education, all could be equal. Providing opportunity and education was the job of the "civilization" program. "Civilization" meant something very specific to Knox. Indians must give up their hunting and warring and become peaceful farmers. They must learn to read and write English, wear shirts and trousers or skirts, live in nuclear families on individual homesteads, govern themselves according to republican principles, and become Christians. By abandoning their cultures and embracing American ways of thinking, acting, and working, they would find places in American society and survive as individuals. If they did not, they would disappear, just as the Indians within the borders of the states had disappeared, because "uncivilized" people, he assumed, could not live among the civilized. The plan also promised to achieve the territory necessary for America's future growth. "Civilized" Indians, Knox believed, would realize that selling off their extensive hunting lands made sense for them because it would provide investment capital for their farms and businesses. "Civilization," therefore, was the perfect policy: It benefited both the Indians and the United States.

Knox had little impact on Indian policy under the Articles of Confederation. Although Congress moved to modify its confiscatory actions, the United States continued to acquire and sell to settlers the lands it claimed north of the

Ohio River. The southern states, despite the wars on their borders, were unmoved. As a result, Cherokee warriors, often in concert with allied Creeks, continued to defend their country with attacks on the settlements established illegally on their side of the border. Because the Articles of Confederation recognized the authority of the states over the Indians within their boundaries, there was nothing Knox or Congress could do to end the conflicts.

The Constitution, ratified in 1789, redesigned the federal government and gave it powers it had lacked under the Articles of Confederation. It defined congressional action as superior to state law and granted Congress the exclusive authority to regulate commerce with the tribes. The president, with the advice and consent of the Senate, had the power to make treaties. Knox acted quickly to define the federal role in Indian affairs. Broadly interpreting "commerce" to include all relations with the tribes, he looked to the treaty power, which denied states the right to negotiate treaties. The Senate shared Knox's opinion that agreements with the tribes were treaties according to the constitutional definition. Therefore, he was able to circumvent the states and their aggressive policies and develop treaty relations with the tribes that would keep the peace, secure the lives of frontier Americans, establish a system of orderly expansion, and benefit the Indians by preparing them through education and training for admission into American society.

President Washington embraced Knox's "civilization" policy, and it became official. The United States would recognize tribal sovereignty and the right of Indians to their lands. The federal government would conduct relations with the tribes by treaty negotiation, pay for lands that tribes willingly sold, and define and defend boundaries to prevent illegal settlement by American citizens. The government also would provide livestock, agricultural implements, tools, and instruction so that the Indians could be transformed from hunters to farmers and herders. The administration rested its treaty system on these principles, and Congress incorporated them in the Trade and Intercourse Acts, first enacted in 1790 and expanded frequently in subsequent years.

The Treaty of Hopewell, which the Cherokees had signed in 1785 and which remained in effect after the ratification of the Constitution, had satisfied the demands of neither North Carolina nor Georgia, both of which vigorously protested its failure to acquire all the Cherokee lands they desired. Furthermore, the treaty described a boundary for the Cherokee Nation and proclaimed the lands within it off-limits to settlement. In violation of the treaty but with the approbation of the states, thousands of Americans crossed into the Cherokee Nation, fought off Cherokee efforts to exercise their treaty right to oust them, and called out to the United States for protection and annexation. Knox termed this state-supported encroachment "disgraceful."[2] Fearful that the troubles would explode into full-scale war and unwilling to expel the offending squatters, in 1791 the Washington administration negotiated the Treaty of Holston with the Cherokee Nation. The government induced the Cherokees to sell a large tract on which most of the squatters lived, pledged to survey a new boundary, renewed the provision of the Hopewell treaty that authorized the Cherokees to "punish . . . as they please" any future squatters, and promised to pay an annuity, an annual cash sum, for the cession. Rewarding the squatters by purchasing from the Cherokees the land they had occupied illegally set a pernicious precedent.[3] Intruders learned that they could get away with violating the boundaries that supposedly protected Indian lands. Continued encroachments and the consequent fear of violence led to additional treaties in 1794 and 1798. In each case, the Cherokee Nation surrendered tracts that had been occupied by American squatters who complained that their lives were threatened by Cherokee warriors and argued that only quick action by the United States could preclude a general war. The role of prominent politicians, such as Governor William Blount of Tennessee, in land speculation only exacerbated the situation.

In accord with Knox's plan, the Treaty of Holston included a provision that promised the "implements of husbandry" necessary for the Cherokees to become "herdsmen and cultivators."[4] Under the terms of the treaty the Cherokees received hundreds of plows, hoes, axes, spinning wheels, looms, and other equipment considered essential to "civilized" life. They readily accepted these goods because they were in dire straits. In the second half of the eighteenth century, armies, militias, and finally squatters had invaded their country. Furthermore, the deerskin trade on which the colonial Cherokee economy had depended was in sharp decline.

Overhunting had depleted deer herds and free-range live-stock owned by squatters destroyed the deer's habitat. The Cherokees realized that their future depended on adopting new ways of making a living as well as preserving an amicable relationship with the United States.

In 1792 President Washington appointed an agent to take up residence in the Cherokee Nation to provide instruction in "civilization." The agent acted as a liaison between the federal government and the Cherokees, and the president expected him to promote United States interests, including the cession of land. Some agents became closely aligned with the people they served: The Cherokees' first agent, for example, married a Cherokee woman, defended the Cherokees against Blount and other speculators, and lost his job. The next agent was loyal primarily to Blount. But other agents, especially Silas Dinsmoor and Return J. Meigs, were more conscientious in performance of their duties—even though their goal was the same. They employed blacksmiths, millers, and other Americans whose skills the Cherokees needed in their economic transformation, and they tried to protect Cherokee territory from encroachment, all the while looking for opportunities to promote the sale of land they considered to be unused and surplus.

The United States agency was located at Southwest Point until 1807 and then at Hiwassee Town; both were on the border of the Cherokee Nation and Tennessee and adjacent to the United States factory. The factory was a trading post operated by the government that sold goods to the Cherokees at fair prices. Among some tribes, the factory used the extension of credit to entrap Indian customers in debt that only land cessions could erase, but the Cherokee factory sought primarily to turn Cherokees into consumers who valued material goods. Knox believed that the factory's inventory was a powerful inducement to cultural change. As individuals purchased goods at the factory, they gradually would come to regard their land as a commodity to be bought and sold. The factory, therefore, was a first step toward inculcating "a love for exclusive property," which Knox thought was essential to Cherokee "civilization" and peaceful land acquisition.[5] The factory, however, was largely superfluous, for Cherokees had been trading with Europeans for a century, and a number of Cherokee traders operated their own stores at more accessible locations. By 1811 Cherokee merchants competed so successfully with the government factory that the United States decided to close it.

Thomas Jefferson, who became president in 1801, shared the Enlightenment beliefs of Knox, Washington, and others that Indians were capable of learning "civilization" and, with training, entering American society. He therefore supported Knox's "civilization" policy, and during his presidency he authorized the negotiation of many treaties that contained provisions for supplying the tribes with the same kinds of goods and services that marked the agreements of the 1790s. But Jefferson was also frustrated by the "civilization" policy. It had not convinced the Indians that selling land to the United States was good for them. Land had not become available to

American settlers as rapidly as they wished, so it had not kept the peace. Finally, the Indians, though eager to learn from Americans, were rarely willing to abandon their cultures completely in favor of the ways of Americans. Put simply, too many "uncivilized" Indians held too much land off the market.

Jefferson believed that the future of the republic depended on the speedy acquisition of land to supply its rapidly growing population, and the future of the Indians depended on their dispossession. In his scale of priorities, acquiring land ranked higher than "civilizing" Indians, but like Knox, he linked the two. Jefferson's "civilizing" and negotiating tactics, however, were far more aggressive than anything Knox had envisioned. Jefferson was convinced that depriving Indians of their hunting grounds was in their best interest because it would force them to become "civilized." He ordered his agents to intensify the pressure on the tribes to sell more and larger tracts of land, and he let it be known that threats, intimidation, and bribery were acceptable tactics to get the job done. The Cherokees were one of the targeted tribes because Tennessee, admitted to statehood in 1796, contained a great deal of Cherokee land within its borders, and many of its leading men were deeply involved in land speculation. In four treaties concluded between 1804 and 1806 the Cherokee Nation parted with huge blocks of land in the central and southwest parts of the state. Despite the new emphasis on land sales introduced by Jefferson, however, "civilization" remained an integral part of the Indian policy of the United States.[6]

On the eve of Jefferson's election, a new force for "civiliz-ing" the Cherokees emerged—Christian missionaries. Two Moravians from Salem, North Carolina, had journeyed to the Nation in 1799 to request permission to open a mission, and the next year, the Cherokees consented. The chiefs made it clear, however, that they wanted education for their children, not Christianity, and when the missionaries were slow to start a school, the chiefs threatened expulsion. In the meantime, they permitted a Presbyterian minister in east Tennessee to open a school in 1804 (and a second in 1806), and later that year the Moravians began teaching a few children at Spring Place in what is today north Georgia. The Presbyterian effort endured for seven years; the Moravians remained until re-moval and then rejoined the Cherokees in the West. Neither had much success converting the Cherokees. The Moravians had been in the Nation for a decade before they baptized their first convert, their neighbor Peggy Scott, widow of the promi-nent headman James Vann. Four years later, they admitted Charles Hicks, who later became principal chief.

Following the War of 1812, Methodists and Baptists as well as the American Board of Commissioners for Foreign Missions entered the Cherokee mission field. The American Board was an interdenominational organization headquar-tered in Boston and composed mainly of Congregationalists and Presbyterians. Like the Methodists and Baptists, the American Board drew its spiritual energy from the wave of revivalism that swept the United States in the early nine-teenth century. Sometimes called the Second Awakening (the first had been in the 1740s), this evangelical movement sought the perfection of society through religion. Its adherents believed that the conversion of non-Christians around the world was not only desirable but possible, perhaps in as little as ten years. Evangelicalism linked spiritual and secular life, and influenced by the movement, Congress established the "civilization" fund in 1819 to support missionary efforts. Missionaries taught not merely reading, writing, and arithmetic but also farming, housekeeping, personal grooming, table manners, and other skills that they believed constituted "civilized" life. On one level, they were not very successful—by removal only about 10 percent of Cherokees had joined Christian churches—but in terms of "civilization," they made greater inroads.

Unlike the agent who lived at the edge of the Cherokee Nation, the missions were located throughout the Nation, and the missionaries provided daily lessons on how they believed Cherokees should live. They planted wheat, a "civilized" crop, in their fields in addition to corn, which they regarded with some disdain as "savage." Men cultivated the fields with horses and plows, unlike most Cherokee farming in which women hoed their crops of corn, beans, and squash. Women took care of the housekeeping, laundry, sewing, and cooking. Both men and women dressed modestly, without ostentatious displays of jewelry. Missionaries kept regular mealtimes, and, in a clear violation of the Cherokees' hospitality ethic, some did their best to avoid feeding Cherokees who dropped by uninvited. They disapproved of the Cherokee ball game and other practices that they regarded as "heathen," and they tried to prevent the parents of their students from resorting to traditional medicine to treat their children's illnesses. Their ethnocentrism offends modern sensibilities, but most Cherokees recognized it for what it was. Comfortable with their own cultural orientation, Cherokees took full advantage of the lessons they found useful and ignored those that they did not. Usually Cherokees and missionaries forged a cooperative relationship.[7] A good example is the printing press for their bilingual newspaper, the *Cherokee Phoenix*. The Cherokee Council provided the funds, and the American Board made arrangements for the purchase of the press and types in both English and the syllabary invented by Sequoyah. The Nation used the press to print the newspaper, and the missionaries used it to print Cherokee hymnals and translations of parts of the Bible.[8]

Cherokees had incorporated the deerskin trade into their culture in the eighteenth century, and now they moved to incorporate "civilization." By the end of the eighteenth century a number of Cherokees had accumulated substantial capital. Some had inherited trading posts from European fathers and grandfathers; others had been particularly successful hunters; and still others had acquired considerable wealth through raiding. Now they began to look for ways to invest that capital. They constructed toll roads and ferries, opened inns to serve the traveling public, and bought livestock and equipment. The one thing that they did not buy was land, because the Cherokees continued to own their land in common. Each Cherokee could clear and cultivate as much land as he or she wished as long as that use did not infringe on the rights of others. For Cherokees who sought wealth, labor was the controlling factor, and, because land was available to all, few Cherokees were willing to work for wages. Consequently, some Cherokee planters brought in white families as sharecroppers until the agent put a stop to what he viewed as an unseemly racial inversion. Others purchased African-American slaves to work their fields.[9]

The acquisition of slave labor illustrates the complexity of cultural change. Traditionally women had farmed and men had hunted. Proponents of "civilization" sought to turn men into farmers and women into housewives, but they met solid resistance. Most men flatly refused to engage in farming between spring tilling with horse and plow and harvest. Instead, they engaged in commerce, herded livestock, and bought others to do their farming for them. In wealthy households, women did not cultivate the commercial fields, but most still kept kitchen gardens from which their family's food came. In more culturally conservative families, women did the farming while men herded the livestock that had replaced game. Any shift in gender roles before removal, therefore, was more apparent than real.[10] Although proponents of "civilization" failed on this score, the expanding material culture of the wealthy should have been encouraging if indeed consumerism paved the way to land cession. Once again, the result was unanticipated. Cherokee planters recognized that the practice of holding land in common freed capital for investment elsewhere. Therefore, they became even more committed to preserving the common title to land and resisted any attempt to allot the Cherokee domain to individuals. They also began to take steps to preserve their land base from sale by self-interested individuals.

Cherokees had begun to centralize their government in the eighteenth century in order to prevent young warriors from raiding the frontier and provoking retribution on innocent Cherokees. In the late 1790s the council began to take on responsibilities for internal order that once had rested with clans. A police force, later called the Light Horse Guard, was established to suppress horse-stealing. A law passed in 1808 empowered the Light Horse to defend the bequests of a few wealthy men to their wives and children against matrilineal relatives who sought to preserve more traditional patterns of inheritance. The vast majority of Cherokees followed old lines of descent and had little personal property for the Light Horse to guard, but they supported the centralization of Cherokee government because it seemed to be the best way to protect the common title to their homeland and their integrity as a nation.

Events in the first decade of the nineteenth century sorely tested the Cherokees' commitment to a unified nation. Old chiefs seemed not to grasp the dangers inherent in the cozy new relationship with the United States, and they tended to think in terms of their towns rather than the Nation. Some appeared to be entirely too self-serving, a legacy perhaps of the individualistic ethos of warriors. At this time, the Cherokee Nation was informally divided into the Lower Towns, which included the region of Chickamauga resistance in northeastern Alabama, and the Upper Towns of east Tennessee that encompassed many people who had left their traditional towns in the aftermath of invasions and cessions to settle in northwest Georgia. The United States agent, Return J. Meigs, tended to manipulate the Lower Town chiefs with bribes and special considerations. In 1806, for example, a group of Lower Town chiefs led by Doublehead ceded the last Cherokee hunting grounds. A number of Cherokee chiefs received private reservations, that is, fee simple title, to land within the ceded area, which many leased to Americans and held for speculation. President Jefferson gave Doublehead, in addition to a reservation, one thousand dollars for his role in the cession. Several young chiefs, including Charles Hicks, The Ridge (later known as Major Ridge), and James Vann, demanded that such actions end and that future treaties be submitted to the Cherokee people for their approval. Doublehead and other Lower Town chiefs showed little evidence of mending their ways, so in August 1807, three Cherokees, including The Ridge, killed Doublehead as punishment for his nefarious dealings and as a warning to others.

Meigs then embarked on a campaign to convince the

Lower Towns to cede their entire territory and move to Arkansas. Meigs had developed serious misgivings about the "civilization" program and increasingly believed that the only way for the Cherokees "to preserve their national existence" was to surrender their homeland and move west.[11] In 1808 the National Council replaced Principal Chief Black Fox, who sided with the Lower Towns, with Second Chief Pathkiller, who opposed the exchange and removal. They also expelled three Lower Town chiefs and appointed additional members to a delegation that was already on its way to Washington to make a treaty. The new delegates arrived in time to thwart this effort, but President Jefferson promised those who wanted to emigrate that the United States would arrange an exchange of eastern Cherokee land for new lands in the West. Upon the delegation's return to the Cherokee Nation, a number of Lower Town Cherokees moved to Arkansas with Meigs's assistance, but the title to the land they settled was unclear. Their departure, however, eased the internal pressure for removal. In 1809 the National Council united in opposition to an exchange of land and wholesale removal and restored Black Fox to the office of principal chief.[12]

The Cherokees then restructured their government. The Council established a National Committee of thirteen members to manage the Nation's affairs and to report to the annual meeting of the National Council. The Committee soon insisted that the Nation's annuity, the United States' annual payment for lands that had been ceded, be paid to them in cash not goods so that they could be sure that they were not being cheated or subsidizing emigration. The headmen denied the right of emigrants to sell their farms to Americans and reaffirmed the principle that the homeland belonged to the Nation. In 1810 the Council went further: It condemned those who had emigrated to the West and stripped them of their citizenship in the Cherokee Nation. They were guilty of "committing treason against the motherland."[13]

The Cherokees continued to strengthen their government in an effort to avoid land cessions. The independent actions of a group of elderly chiefs following the War of 1812 and Meigs's mishandling of their annuity led to further consolidation of power in the hands of the National Committee. In 1817 the Cherokees met "to deliberate and consider on the situation of the Nation, in the disposition of our common property of lands, without the consent of the members of the Council, in order to obviate the evil consequences resulting in such a course." They agreed to a written "Articles of Government," their first constitution, that provided for the election and terms of Committee members and asserted that "the acts of this body shall not be binding on the Nation in our common property and without the unanimous consent of the members and Chiefs of the Council." People who moved out of the Nation lost any claim to common property, and a woman retained her property in the East if her husband emigrated. The document affirmed the right of the Committee to receive the annuity and the requirement that it report to the Council.[14] The Articles of Government failed to prevent additional land cessions in 1817 and 1819, which the United

States demanded in order to provide for an equivalent tract of land for those Cherokees who had emigrated to Arkansas. Following these cessions, however, the Cherokee Nation ceded no more land in the East.

Mindful of the threat to their homeland, the Cherokees confirmed their earlier principles of government in 1825 "for the better security of the common property of the Cherokee Nation, and for the rights and privileges of the Cherokee people."[15] The next year the Council provided for the election of delegates to a constitutional convention, which met in July 1827 and drafted a much more elaborate constitution that strengthened the position of principal chief. The constitution also connected more clearly than ever polity and place. Unlike the constitution of the United States, which provided for expansion, the Cherokee constitution set forth in detail "the boundaries of this Nation, embracing the lands solemnly guarantied and reserved forever to the Cherokee Nation by the Treaties concluded with the United States." Within their Nation's boundaries, the Cherokees expected their government "to establish justice, promote our common welfare, and secure to ourselves and our posterity the blessings of liberty."[16] These goals must have sounded familiar to other Americans.

For an Indian tribe to write a constitution with words echoing the United States Constitution should have marked the triumph of "civilization." But the Cherokees had not dissolved their separate political existence and melded into the

United States population. They had not ceded their land and moved west. They had preserved both their national identity and their homeland. "Civilized and enlightened," they were far better equipped to defend both than they had been when Knox designed the "civilization" program. "Civilization" had not solved the Indian problem after all.

3

INDIAN REMOVAL POLICY

"WE BELIEVE the present plan of the General Government to effect our removal West of the Mississippi, and thus obtain our lands for the use of the state of Georgia, to be highly oppressive, cruel, and unjust," wrote a group of Cherokee women to the *Cherokee Phoenix* in 1831.[1] In the twentieth century similar government policies of expelling one people to make room for another have been called "ethnic cleansing." No one thought of such a harsh term in the early nineteenth century—people preferred an antiseptic, impersonal one like "removal," even though to the Indians there was nothing impersonal about it. In one sense, removal was a continuation of the policies created by Europeans when they first came to America, took a piece of land, and pushed the Indians off it so they could use it for themselves. Indian policy had always been about getting the land and getting rid of the Indians who lived on it. People did not call these actions removal, but they were, nevertheless. In another sense, however, the removal policy of the 1820s and 1830s was a revolutionary program of political and social engineering that caused unimaginable suffering, deaths in the thousands, and emotional pain that lingers to this day. The words "oppressive, cruel, and unjust" do not capture its horror.

The most obvious thing about the removal policy is that it was a rejection of the "civilization" policy. Knox had developed the "civilization" policy in the first place because the Indians had rejected the conquered-nations policy of the 1780s. George Washington and Thomas Jefferson had embraced "civilization" in part because they thought they were providing a future for the Indians. Many Indians, especially the Cherokees, found much to admire in American culture, and they liked the idea of having a future, so they studied hard and learned well. But they also found much of value in their own culture, and they wanted *their* future, not Knox's. The Cherokees used the "civilization" policy to empower themselves so that they could better defend their country and resist the United States. But in their resistance, they cast doubt on the efficacy of the "civilization" policy. If they did not become "civilized" Americans and assimilate into American society, the policy was a failure. It seemed that the Indians, by refusing to become "civilized," were rejecting that policy.

Many Americans agreed that the "civilization" policy was a failure, but they did not think it was simply because the Indians had rejected it. They argued that the "savagery" of the Indians was not the result of their uneducated situation, as Knox and others believed, but because they were, by virtue of their racial inferiority, incapable of learning. Racist explanations for the deficiencies of the Indians had been around for a long time, but until the early nineteenth century, they had rarely overwhelmed the Enlightenment ideas of racial equality and human perfectibility. In conjunction with the sweeping social, intellectual, economic, and political changes that marked the early nineteenth century, however, Americans began to think new things about race and racial categories. In part this change was tied to the emergence of romantic nationalism, the concept that each people has its own inherent national character. In this view, the United States was a white man's country. But it also reflected the growing preoccupation with slavery and its racial justification. In either case, critics agreed that Indians could never become fully "civilized" because it was impossible to redress through education deficiencies that were caused by race. As they were determined by race to be forever "uncivilized," there could never be a place of equality for Indians in American society.

The impossibility of assimilating Indians became a problem because American demands for land steadily reduced the amount of land available to sustain Indian life. Over the preceding generations, as Indian populations had declined and land cessions had carved off tracts that abutted settled areas, the tribes either retained adequate acreage or withdrew to neighboring areas. But since 1814, tribal holdings in the South had been reduced to three islands of Indians—Choctaws and Chickasaws in the Mississippi valley, Cherokees and Creeks farther east, and Seminoles to the south—all surrounded by a sea of Americans. Each cession shrank the islands, the sea of non-Indian settlements threatened to inundate what remained, and the problem of what to do about the remaining Indians became increasingly pressing. The "civilization" policy had provided the answer—detribalized, "civilized" Indians on small family-owned farms would join American society as fully equal citizens. The racist rejection of "civilization" denied that solution to the problem. Governor Joseph McMinn of Tennessee wrote in 1816 that detribalized Indians living in his state would be "entitled to all the rights of a free citizen of color," a limbo of second-class citizenship with virtually no civil rights.[2] George M. Troup, governor of Georgia, elaborated in 1824: "The utmost of rights and privileges which public opinion would concede to Indians would fix them in a middle station, between the negro and white man." So situated, the Indians would "gradually sink to the condition of the former—a point of degeneracy below which they could not fall."[3] By denying Indians the promise of "civilization," McMinn and Troup removed from U.S. policy any pretense of benefit for Indians. Tribal leaders no longer imagined that selling more land would result in advantages for their people. Under such circumstances, they decided to resist with all their ability any additional cessions. By 1822 the Cherokees had resolved "not to dispose of even one foot of ground."[4] For those like McMinn and Troup, who believed that a "civilized" Indian was a contradiction in terms, the only logical solution to the question of what to do with the Indians was to expel them. Such thinking gained credence during the early nineteenth century and fueled the growing interest in replacing the "civilization" policy with removal.

Anti-Indian racism, however, was not confined to the slaveholding South. In the mid-1820s, the citizens of Cornwall, Connecticut, and the directors of the American Board of Commissioners for Foreign Missions, a leading missionary organization active in "civilizing" Indians, betrayed racist opinions that differed little from those held by Georgians. In 1818, two of the most talented and best-educated Cherokee young men, John Ridge and Elias Boudinot, entered the American Board's boarding school at Cornwall. Cousins, they had imbibed all the education the mission schools in the Nation could provide, they hungered for more, and the missionaries selected them for further training. Despite the rules of the school that forbade students free movement around town or association with townspeople, both met and fell in love with young Cornwall women. The parents of both girls were shocked by the confessions of their daughters that they hoped to marry the cousins, but in the end the parents relented, despite the hostility of the local clergy and press. John Ridge and Sarah Bird Northrup married in her home on January 27, 1824, less than a month after Ridge, embittered by the uproar, had published an article in the *Christian Herald* on the racist opinion that "an Indian is almost considered accursed."[5] One local editor, who found the presence of Indian and other nonwhite students in

his neighborhood offensive, pretended to sympathize with the disgrace of Sarah's family because she had "made herself a squaw."[6] Two years later, when word got out that Harriet Gold intended to wed Elias Boudinot, her brother led a mob that burned her in effigy in the town square. When they married, school officials termed their union "criminal." In order to prevent the like from happening again, in the fall of 1826 the American Board closed the school.[7]

The difficulties the two young couples endured had lasting effects. They never abandoned their beliefs in the importance of education for the Cherokees, and they remained dedicated promoters of "civilization," but neither Ridge nor Boudinot entertained any further notions about the entry of "civilized" Cherokees into American society. Rather, they agreed that the Cherokee Nation must endure intact, Cherokee "civilization" must unfold in a national context, and the future happiness of the Cherokee people depended on the preservation of their separate and distinct identity.[8]

Being victimized by racism did not blind Boudinot, who became editor of the *Cherokee Phoenix*, to the complexity of the crisis facing the Cherokees. In one of his editorials he pointed out that there was more than racism at work. "Cupidity and self-interest are at the bottom of all these difficulties. A desire to possess the Indian land is paramount to a desire to see him established on the soil as a civilized man."[9] Boudinot knew and understood the implications of the recent past. The demand for Indian land had never been greater, and the prospects for acquiring it had never seemed better.

[47]

Simultaneously with the War of 1812, the United States fought two wars against western Indians. Both the war in the Great Lakes country against the intertribal alliance system led by Tecumseh and his brother, the Shawnee Prophet, and the one in the South against the Red Stick faction of the Creeks, resulted in crushing American victories. Assessing the meaning of their defeats, Secretary of War John C. Calhoun reported to the House of Representatives in 1818 that the Indians had "ceased to be an object of terror. The time seems to have arrived when our policy towards them should undergo an important change. . . . Our views of their interest, and not their own, ought to govern them."[10] For the first time since independence, the United States did not need to temper its actions toward western Indians with fear of their violent reactions.

The post–War of 1812 period was a time of tremendous, almost comprehensive, change in the United States. Victory over Great Britain for the second time in a generation invigorated the American people with an almost boundless nationalistic enthusiasm. A blossoming transportation revolution, marked by the introduction of steamboats on the western rivers and the development of more efficient highway and canal systems, opened new markets in distant places for western produce. A brief but spectacular spike in prices promised unprecedented prosperity for western farmers. Like a flood of water from an upturned bottle, Americans poured into the western country after the war. Grain and livestock farmers spread north of the Ohio River, Indiana and Illinois became

states in 1816 and 1818, and their combined populations jumped from 37,000 in 1810 to nearly a half million in 1830. South of the Ohio the expansion of cotton plantation agriculture produced the same result. Mississippi and Alabama entered the Union in 1817 and 1819 and their combined populations rose from 40,000 in 1810 to 445,000 in 1830. The older states of Ohio, Tennessee, and Georgia also experienced dramatic growth. Their combined populations were 745,000 in 1810 and over two million in 1830. During the twenty years in which the populations of the western states exploded, Indian nations owned land within the boundaries of all of them. The economic forces that fed this growth generated an unprecedented demand for their land, which was nowhere more intense than in the South. The southern tribes, the Chickasaws, Choctaws, Creeks, and Cherokees in particular, held millions of acres of fertile land that planters hoped to turn into cotton fields. The cotton plantation system that dominated the southern states depended on the labor of African-American slaves, and southerners defined and justified that system in racial terms. The result was that southerners were peculiarly responsive to Troup's argument that Indians, like blacks, were racially inferior and therefore incapable of "civilization." Racism, coupled with Calhoun's arrogance and the "cupidity and self-interest" that Boudinot described, formed a powerful combination against the Indians.

Andrew Jackson became a central figure in this threatening coalition. He had commanded the army that defeated the Red Stick Creeks in 1814, and later that year he had dictated a peace treaty that forced the Creek Nation to surrender some twenty million acres of land in Alabama and Georgia. During the next few years the government appointed him to negotiate four additional treaties with the southern Indian nations. Jackson did not like the work. Mostly he did not like bargaining with Indians. It meant that he had to sit and listen to them refuse his demands and make counterproposals. The tribes were not sovereign, he claimed, and to pretend that they were by negotiating treaties with them was "absurd." They were within the boundaries of the United States, and the government should treat them as subjects, not as sovereigns. Negotiating treaties with the tribes might have made sense in the old days when they were strong and the United States was weak, but "circumstances have entirely changed," he wrote President James Monroe early in 1817, and "the arm of government [is] sufficiently strong to carry [a new policy] into execution." Denying the right of the tribes to land ownership as well as their sovereignty, Jackson argued that Congress should simply enact legislation to take their land.[11]

Jackson did not invent the scheme to relocate Indians to the country west of the Mississippi River, but he was recommending it in his capacity as negotiator of treaties with southern Indians. The idea came to Thomas Jefferson in 1803, shortly after the purchase of Louisiana, and Return J. Meigs, agent to the Cherokee Nation, raised it with some of the Nation's leaders the next year. In 1809 Jefferson, at Meigs's recommendation, suggested to a delegation of Cherokees in

Washington that they should give serious consideration to relocating in the West. Viewing this as an opportunity to escape from the problem of encroachment and harassment by frontier Americans, a few Cherokees accepted the idea and moved to land north of the Arkansas River. But the idea of fleeing to the West attracted no more than a thousand Cherokees, despite Meigs's repeated efforts to convince them. Following the interlude of the War of 1812, the government renewed its efforts to acquire land from the Cherokee Nation, and Jackson, McMinn, and Meigs encouraged the Cherokees to exchange their lands in the East for a new country in the West. This time, two thousand went. Treaties with the Choctaw Nation in 1820 and the Creek Nation in 1826 contained similar suggestions, but like the Cherokees they were not enthusiastic about removal and only small numbers of people moved.

While nearly all in government agreed that the United States needed to acquire more land from the Indian tribes to accommodate its growing population and booming economy, there was no agreement on how they should do it. In 1818, the House Committee on Public Lands rejected Jackson's suggestion of using the power of eminent domain to condemn Indian land for public use, stating that the treaty system was well established and should be continued. That same year Congress defeated a bill to appropriate money to pay for the removal of Indians to the West on the grounds that U.S. policy was to "civilize" the Indians where they were. Those who wished to migrate would have to go as individuals and pay their own way. In 1819 Congress reaffirmed its dedication to "civilization" with the passage of a law that appropriated ten thousand dollars per year to subsidize the "civilization" efforts of mission groups. In the next five years, this money financed the opening of twenty-one new schools in Indian country.

President James Monroe, like many in government after the War of 1812, embraced both "civilization" and removal. By 1818 removal was the "great object" of his administration, largely because he saw it as the only way to protect the Indians from the political and moral decay that he considered the inevitable result of being surrounded by American settlements. Monroe's successor, John Quincy Adams, held much the same opinion. Even as they convinced themselves that removal was the only way to save the Indians, they rejected absolutely any suggestion that removal should be made mandatory. Congress agreed. Throughout the 1820s, removal remained a voluntary option, a corollary to "civilization," and the message from Washington was that it would continue to regard Indian tribes as sovereign nations with the power to decide when, if, and under what circumstances they would cede lands. U.S. Indian policy thus continued to pursue Knox's original expectation that the Indians, once "civilized," would understand that they no longer needed their hunting lands and would willingly sell them for investment capital. Presumably they would also be able to decide where they wanted to live.

While Congress clung to "civilization," growing numbers

of American citizens not only demanded more land from the tribes, they took it. The illegal occupation of Indian land by American squatters was a problem everywhere and had been for generations. The warfare between Indians and intruders had caused the crisis Henry Knox had hoped to solve with his "civilization" policy in the 1790s, and virtually every treaty concluded by American commissioners and tribal leaders included a clause that obligated the United States to defend tribal land rights and expel intruders. But the government found it impolitic to use its troops to evict its citizens from Indian country. It rarely did so, and when it did, the squatters simply returned when the soldiers withdrew. Tribal forces proved the only effective police against intruders, but when they acted, in the case of the Cherokees with treaty authorization, the result was likely to be violent. Intrusion by settlers made normal life in the Cherokee Nation extremely difficult. While tribal leaders never relaxed their efforts to oust the settlers, Cherokee dependence on federal protection of their borders, however ineffectual, was galling.

In the early 1820s, Thomas L. McKenney, the War Department clerk charged with administrative responsibility for U.S. relations with the Indians, began to complain about a brewing "crisis in Indian affairs." The crisis had two causes. One was the development of tribal nationalism; the other was the emerging doctrine of state rights. In the relations of the Cherokee Nation with Georgia, these two collided in the 1820s with explosive force.

Emergent Cherokee nationalism during the first third of the nineteenth century is evident in the innovative alterations in governmental institutions engineered by Cherokee political leaders. It is most easily charted, however, in the increasingly shrill warnings contained in the correspondence of their federal Indian agent, Return J. Meigs. As early as 1811, Agent Meigs informed Washington of the "erroneous ideas of their distinct sovereignty & independence" crystallizing among the Cherokees. If not nipped in the bud, Meigs predicted, such "false ideas of their national independence" would only grow.[12] And grow they did. Meigs repeated his warning in 1817 in the wake of the treaty negotiation and general refusal of the Cherokees to migrate west. In 1822, when the Cherokee National Council refused to meet with U.S. commissioners charged with opening talks on another land cession, Meigs called its decision a "declaration of independence which they never lose sight of."[13] Two years later, in an argument with Secretary Calhoun about Georgia's claims to their lands, a Cherokee delegation to Washington pointed out that, contrary to Georgia's assertions, they were not the foreigners and intruders on the land. The country had been theirs long before the establishment of Georgia. In a nice reversal of Georgia's pretensions, the delegates also declared that they "cannot recognize the sovereignty of any State within the limits of their territory."[14] The ultimate expression of Cherokee nationalism came in 1827 with the drafting of the Nation's constitution. In defining the boundaries of the Cherokee Nation and announcing the sovereignty of the

Nation within them, the Cherokees carried their ideas of sovereignty and independence to their logical and most threatening conclusion.

Georgia's reaction to the promulgation of the Cherokee constitution was apoplectic. But apoplectic reactions to the festering questions of Indian land rights and its claims to them was no new thing for Georgia. Georgia's history, as colony and state, is littered with conflicts with Native nations over land. The Creek Nation was its target more often than the Cherokees, but neither escaped the continual demands of Georgia for more land.

After 1802, Georgia cited its compact with the United States to justify its actions. In that year Georgia followed the example of Virginia and North Carolina and surrendered to the federal government its charter claims to its western lands, the region that later became Alabama and Mississippi. In return for this grant, the United States paid $1.25 million and issued the promise that it would extinguish the Indian title to the land within the newly established boundaries of Georgia "as soon as the same can be peaceably obtained on reasonable terms."[15] Following the conclusion of the 1819 treaty with the Cherokees, which netted the state no land at all, the Georgia General Assembly addressed a petition to Congress that charged the federal government with bad faith. The government was under obligation to no other state to clear the Indian claims within its borders, complained the legislature, but while other states received land from the Indians, Georgia did not. Since 1802 the state had waited patiently, but to no avail, and Georgia was losing patience. Other petitions followed, reinforced by resolutions and bills presented to Congress by Georgia's congressmen and senators. All cited the Compact of 1802 and decried the failure of the government to meet its obligation. Not only had Washington paid more attention to the less legitimate expectations of other states, it had persisted in concluding treaties that guaranteed tribal rights to their lands, thereby reinforcing tribal resistance to additional demands for land.

One of Georgia's petitions charging bad faith, received by the House of Representatives late in 1822, led to an investigation by a special committee chaired by George Gilmer, a Georgian. Not surprisingly, the committee reported that the government had indeed failed to fulfill its legal and moral responsibility to Georgia and called on the president for a report. President Monroe submitted a statement March 30, 1823, in which he recounted the efforts of his and previous administrations to purchase for Georgia the Indian land within its boundaries. Georgia had gained a great deal over the previous twenty years, he pointed out, but the Cherokee Nation had refused to sell any more. "In their present temper they can be removed only by force, . . . and there is no obligation on the United States to remove the Indians by force." Indeed, "an attempt to remove them by force would be, in my opinion, unjust." Monroe believed that the Cherokees would be better off if they moved away, and he would continue to advise them to do so, but until they made the decision themselves there was nothing further the federal government could do. In other words, the president denied the charge by Georgia and the House committee that the United States had acted in bad faith toward the state. Furthermore, he rejected Georgia's demand that the government should act in bad faith toward the Indians.[16] Most important, he recognized that the Cherokee Nation had the sovereign right to refuse to sell. Monroe then sent a special message to Congress urging that body to enact legislation authorizing the government to negotiate the exchange of all Indian lands in the East for comparable amounts in the West. Explaining this as a measure necessary to the survival of the Indians, he expressed confidence that tribal leaders understood their critical situation and would readily agree to such a proposal. John Quincy Adams, Monroe's successor in the White House, followed suit with a similar recommendation to Congress.

Congress acted on none of these proposals, leaving an opening for action by the interested states. By 1826, Georgia's efforts had largely achieved the expulsion of the Creek Nation. Success had taught Georgia's politicians that a program of stubborn persistence, bluster, and the threat of civil conflict could intimidate the federal government into action. Thus emboldened, they turned their undivided attention toward the Cherokee Nation and the nearly five million acres it held in northwest Georgia. Their campaign began in December 1826, with a resolution of the General Assembly that called on the president, once again, to remove the remaining Indians from the state. In 1827, following the drafting of the Cherokee constitution and the failure of the federal government to condemn it, the Assembly enacted a more comprehensive resolution. Denouncing the Cherokee constitution as outrageous and claiming that the establishment of a sovereign Cherokee republic was unconstitutional, the legislature announced that Georgia had sovereignty over all the lands within its boundaries and asserted that it could take possession of the country occupied by Indians whenever and by whatever means it pleased. The politicians pledged to use violence only as a last resort, but Georgians vowed that, if the government failed to fulfill the terms of the Compact of 1802, they would do whatever was necessary. To justify their thinly veiled threat of force, the legislators adopted the cry, "The lands in question belong to Georgia. She *must* and she *will* have them."[17] With this resolution claiming sovereignty, the Georgia legislature challenged the constitutional authority of the federal government to control relations with the tribes, denied the validity of the treaties that recognized tribal sovereignty and land rights, and asserted with undeniable clarity its claims to sovereign power.

The next year, with no treaty concluded with the Cherokee Nation, the Georgia Assembly revisited the question of the relationship between the state and the land of the Cherokees. In a law to go into effect June 1, 1830, the legislature extended the civil and criminal jurisdiction of the state into the region owned and occupied by the Cherokees, subjecting the Indians to Georgia law but denying them the right to testify in court against a white person. At the same time, the legislature declared that all laws and actions of the Cherokee government were null and void, "as if the same had never existed." Alabama followed suit in 1829.[18]

While Georgia played a significant role in the transition from a policy of "civilization" to one of removal, historians commonly identify the policy with Andrew Jackson. He won the presidency in 1828 by a substantial margin, and the voters who resided in states that had large Indian populations were well aware of Jackson's views about Indians and their future in the United States. Tribes were not sovereign, Indians were subjects, and the government should treat them accordingly. Conducting treaty negotiations with the tribes to purchase their land was absurd. And unless individual Indians wanted to live in the states as second-class citizens, they should go west. Though not original to Jackson, these ideas matured during the 1820s, and when coupled with the developing crisis in Indian affairs that McKenney had dreaded, they formed Jackson's Indian policy.

Jackson detailed the removal policy in his first annual message, delivered to Congress on December 8, 1829. He opened by discussing the crisis generated by the Cherokee constitution and the extension of jurisdiction by Georgia and Alabama. These conflicting sovereignties had appealed to the government for resolution, but to Jackson the proper course was clear. The Constitution prohibited the erection of one state within the boundaries of another without the agreement of the latter. Neither Georgia nor Alabama agreed to the establishment of a Cherokee republic; therefore, it was unconstitutional, and the Cherokees must give it up. This left the

Cherokees two choices, "emigrate beyond the Mississippi" or "submit to the laws of those States." Jackson then condemned all the suffering and death that "this much-injured race" had experienced at the hands of Europeans and Americans and predicted that, if he did not act quickly to protect them, mistreatment would continue, and the Indians would be destroyed. His solution for saving them was removal. Congress should set aside a country west of the Mississippi, to be guaranteed to the tribes, where they could govern themselves free from interference. The "benevolent" could continue their efforts at "civilization" there, and someday perhaps the Indians could "raise up an interesting commonwealth, destined to perpetuate the race." Removal should be voluntary, he announced, but the Indians must understand that, if they remained in the states, they would be subject to state law. Pretending that most of the Native people in question were wandering hunters rather than village-dwelling farmers, Jackson belittled the claims of the tribes to national domains by insisting that they claimed "tracts of country on which they have neither dwelt nor made improvements, merely because they have seen them from the mountain or passed them in the chase."[19] Those who believed such misleading statements could easily agree that the claims of the tribes were illegitimate.

Jackson had made his program plain. Tribal sovereignty east of the Mississippi was a dead idea. State rights trumped tribal rights, both to government and land, and tribes no longer had the right to refuse either to sell land or to submit to state law. Treaty guarantees to the contrary would be ignored. Only detribalized, "civilized" individual Indians could remain in the East, where they would be subject to the laws of the states in which they lived, even if those laws denied them basic civil liberties. And the only land they could hold was the farm they owned. There could be no sovereign tribes, no tribal governments, no commonly held tribal lands in the East.

Removal was the first legislative recommendation Jackson sent to Congress. It was presented as a key administrative measure, and party leaders in Congress, which was controlled by the Democrats, made its passage a matter of party discipline. By the same token, the opposing National Republican Party geared up to kill it. The House and Senate Committees on Indian Affairs, both of which were dominated by southern Democrats, reported bills that were nearly identical, the House accepted the Senate version, and the Senate took it up first. Led by Senator Theodore Frelinghuysen of New Jersey, opponents spoke first.

Frelinghuysen and those who joined him were well armed with arguments. For a year, public interest in the northern states, which thought about removal in terms of the Cherokee Nation and Georgia, had been focused on defeating the measure. Jeremiah Evarts, the chief administrative officer of the American Board of Commissioners for Foreign Missions, had taken the lead. In a series of twenty-four essays published between August and December 1829 in the Washington *National Intelligencer* under the pen name William

Penn, Evarts attacked removal by defending the rights of the Cherokees and condemning the claims of Georgia. On legal grounds, Evarts argued that U.S. recognition of the sovereignty of the Cherokee Nation had been affirmed repeatedly in treaties, which, as the supreme law of the land, were superior in legal force to Georgia's counterclaims to sovereignty. Refusing to act on the binding obligations written into the treaties to protect the Cherokees from Georgia's aggression, particularly its unconstitutional extension of jurisdiction into the Cherokee Nation, was, Everts claimed, immoral as well as illegal. Embracing a policy that would forcibly expel the Indians to the West simply compounded the immorality.[20] Like-minded people, such as Catherine Beecher, a prominent educator and writer, joined in the fight by encouraging women to organize petition drives urging Congress to reject removal. In a significant moment in the emergent women's movement, women throughout the North followed her lead and swamped Congress with hundreds of petitions containing hundreds of thousands of names.[21] When the Senate debate began, a copy of Evarts's Penn essays published in book form was on every senator's desk. Frelinghuysen, who delivered a speech that lasted three days, relied on those arguments.

John Forsyth, former governor of Georgia, led the response to Frelinghuysen and the enemies of removal. Nothing in the bill provided for removal by force, he explained, and charges that the supporters of removal intended to achieve it forcibly were both hypocritical and an example of antisouthern bias. The northern states had already expelled their Indians, and now they wanted to deny Georgia and her southern sisters the same opportunity to prosper. Like New York and the New England states, Georgia should never have to "submit to the intrusive sovereignty of a petty tribe of Indians." Charging that Indians were a "useless and burdensome" people, the members of a "race not admitted to be equal" to whites and "probably never to be entitled, to equal civil and political rights," Forsyth proclaimed that they could be "humanely provided for" only in the West. The sole alternative to removal was for the Cherokees and the other tribes to surrender their claims to national sovereignty and self-government and submit to the laws of the states in which they lived.[22]

Frelinghuysen and others submitted amendments requiring that neither force nor fraud be used to achieve removal, but they failed. The Senate debate began on April 7; the bill came to a vote on April 24. By an almost straight party line vote it passed by a margin of twenty-eight to nineteen.

Debate in the House of Representatives lasted thirteen days. The opposition arguments, like those in the Senate, depended on the William Penn essays. Supporters followed Forsyth's lead but with added emphasis on the unconstitutionality of *imperium in imperio*, the erection of a Cherokee state within Georgia. The outcome was a much closer 102 to 97. For some northern Democrats, particularly from Pennsylvania and the states of the Ohio valley, party loyalty gave way under the pressure from many of their constituents who opposed removal. But having passed in both houses, the removal bill went to President Jackson for signature.

The act authorized the president to set aside a region west of the states and territories, to divide the region into districts, and to offer each tract to an eastern tribe willing to accept an exchange and move. Congress pledged to guarantee the new homelands to each tribe and offered to issue a patent to the land if the tribe so requested. In return for accepting the exchange, Congress offered to pay compensation for individually owned improvements abandoned in the East, to finance the removal, and to provide support for the people for their first year in the West. The act empowered the president to exercise the same administrative responsibility for managing relations with the removed tribes and assured that nothing in the law "shall be construed as authorizing or directing the violation of any existing treaty." To cover the cost of implementing the act, Congress appropriated five hundred thousand dollars. Jackson signed the bill into law May 28, 1830.[23]

Politicians in later years remembered the House and Senate debates over Jackson's removal bill during the spring of 1830 as the most contentious, protracted, acrimonious, and bitter of their careers. Martin Van Buren, Jackson's vice president and successor, believed that removal was the single most important accomplishment of Jackson's presidency. For the Cherokee Nation, it was the most disastrous piece of congressional legislation, before the 1890s and allotment, in the history of its relations with the United States. While the Democratic Party achieved its passage, the narrowness of the House vote suggests that perhaps half of the American people opposed removal.

Many Democrats believed that opposition stemmed from partisan hostility to Jackson, and the behavior of National Republican politicians who represented states that would benefit from removal suggests that they were, in part, correct.[24] Henry Clay, planning to run against Jackson in 1832, actively opposed the removal policy in hopes of breaking Democratic power in Pennsylvania. Van Buren also explained opposition to removal in partisan terms, but at the same time he recognized that religion played a decisive role. Evarts, Frelinghuysen, and the American Board all reflected an enormously important new force in American society that can best be described as a moral alternative to the kind of romantic nationalism that defined the Jacksonian movement. It was an ethos of restraint and responsibility, a dedication to principles that emphasized justice and honor, a belief that nations, like people, must behave honestly, be faithful to their promises, dedicate their actions to doing good. To people like Evarts, the fight over removal was rooted in the belief that God had chosen the United States to reform a corrupt world, that for it to act unjustly violated God's purpose, and that God would punish the errant nation with disaster if it failed to fulfill its responsibility. Fundamental values were at stake. Supporters of removal were racists, to be sure, and Frelinghuysen accused Forsyth of racism during the debate, but to Evarts and his friends the main problem was that they were grasping opportunists who had turned their backs on the true meaning of God's plan for America.

The American people could accept removal, however,

because that was how it had always been. Whether they had acquired land from the Indians by war or purchase, they had always assumed that the Indians would evacuate it and go somewhere else. And that was the way it should be. Americans did not like to live around Indians. They were "uncivilized," and the effort in recent years to "civilize" them had not worked. Whether they believed that the persistent "savagery" of the Indians was by choice or by racial defect, the fact was that there was no place for "uncivilized" people in "civilized" American society. What made the removal crisis of the 1820s different was that the tribes were surrounded, and they could not simply withdraw quietly as they used to do. Instead, they had to be shipped off in some orchestrated process, and the orchestration was the problem. The debate in Congress, for example, was really about the details. Northern politicians like Frelinghuysen were furious at Georgia because it had legislated the Cherokee Nation out of existence. This was what gave the debate drama. It was less about Indian removal than it was about Cherokee removal. The Cherokees were widely understood to be the most "civilized" Indians in the United States. If there was any tribe that deserved to be praised and petted and left alone on their lands so they could assimilate into American society, it was that one. But Georgia denounced them as "savage," condemned them to second-class citizenship if they entered its society, and demanded with unbridled passion that they surrender their landed wealth. The Removal Act embodied Georgia's assertion that there was no place for Indians in American society and sealed the fate of the Cherokee Nation in two ways. Most obviously, by the end of the 1830s the Cherokee Nation had removed to the West. But perhaps unexpectedly, the Cherokee Nation survived in the West.

JOHN ROSS.
A CHEROKEE CHIEF.

John Ross, who served as principal chief from 1828 to 1866, led the Cherokee Nation's struggle against removal. From Thomas L. McKenney and James Hall, History of the Indian Tribes of North America *(Philadelphia: F. W. Greenough, 1838–44); copy in the Rare Book Collections, Wilson Library, University of North Carolina, Chapel Hill.*

4

RESISTING REMOVAL

"THE CLOUDS MAY GATHER, thunders roar & lightening flash from the acts of Ga. under the approvation of Genl. [Andrew] Jackson's neutrality, but the Cherokees with an honest patriotism & love of country will still remain peaceably and quietly in their own soil." So wrote Principal Chief John Ross in July 1830 to Jeremiah Evarts, author of the antiremoval William Penn essays, and the executive secretary of the American Board of Commissioners for Foreign Missions.[1] The General Assembly of Georgia had passed, and continued to pass, legislation designed to make the lives of the Cherokees so miserable they would welcome the chance to find safety and repose in the West. As their chief, Ross labored to lead the Cherokees through the minefield laid by Georgia and ensure the survival of the sovereign Cherokee Nation in its ancient homeland with its boundaries secure and its people safe in the enjoyment of their property and political rights. Depending on the "honest patriotism & love of country" that filled him with pride in his fellow Cherokees, Ross never deviated from his strategy of peaceable, passive resistance. That it proved insufficient should not detract from the imaginative, daring, and increasingly desperate path down which he led his people.[2]

Georgia's legislation of harassment rested on three motivations. The most powerful was the desire to acquire the nearly five million acres the Cherokee Nation held and refused to sell. Some Georgia politicians dreamed of building a canal through to the Tennessee River and thus giving Georgia access to the vast interior market served by the Ohio-Mississippi River network. But most saw the land as the means to cement their political futures. Unique among the states, Georgia gave away its unoccupied domain in a series of public lotteries. All adult male citizens and widows qualified for a draw, war veterans and other worthies often got two draws, and winning tickets could be sold if the "fortunate drawer" did not wish to take possession of the tract he won. Designed to curb speculation by giving all citizens a chance, the lottery had the effect of demonstrating to Georgians that they, as individuals, could benefit directly from a cession of Cherokee land. The result was that Indian policy was not an abstract issue in Georgia politics. Politicians who claimed to have succeeded in engineering a cession hoped for rewards at the ballot box, which led them to compete with one another in their zeal to acquire land and seize the credit.

Of course, the chance to get a free farm kept the attention of individual Georgians focused on the Indians.

In the racist atmosphere of Georgia, acquiring all the land held by the Cherokee Nation raised the problem of what to do with the Cherokees who lived there. Unwelcome as neighbors, they must be expelled. Georgians understood that they could not simply drive them out. The Cherokees would resist, there might be war, and Georgia would be blamed. Georgians needed some kind of screen to hide behind and cloak their actions with legal respectability. The General Assembly provided that. For example, legislation that denied Cherokees the right to testify in court but subjected them to Georgia law threw open the door to legalized theft of their property, brutalization of their persons, and intimidation of every conceivable kind. Legislation that declared Cherokee law null and void, forbade the Cherokee government to function, and criminalized any public act by Cherokee leaders sought to decapitate the Cherokee Nation and render the Cherokee people helpless. And to cover unexpected contingencies, the General Assembly established the Georgia Guard, a special police force charged to enforce the law that in fact became a central element in the state's program of harassment and intimidation.

Georgia justified its campaign of land grabbing and legal aggression by claiming it had a charter right as one of the original colonies to exercise dominion over all the land and people within its borders. The state pressed this claim against the federal government by insisting that the commerce clause of the U.S. Constitution gave Congress authority to control only trade and left all other relations in the hands of the states. According to this line of argument, any provisions in a treaty that strayed beyond questions of commerce, narrowly defined, were unconstitutional federal usurpations of the sovereign powers of the state. Georgia pressed this claim against the Cherokee Nation as well. Not satisfied to deny the Nation's authority, the state denied its very existence. And when Georgia combined its claim to sovereignty with its argument that treaty provisions guaranteeing land rights to the Cherokees were unconstitutional, it was a short step to the argument that the only right the Indians had to the land they occupied was that of a tenant who could be dispossessed at a moment's notice. The Georgia Assembly waited until 1835 to act on this assertion, but repeatedly asserting it and threatening to act on it proved useful for trying to intimidate the Cherokees.

Georgia's harassment of the Cherokees sometimes reached ludicrous levels. In the early summer of 1831, Governor George Gilmer sent a secret agent into the Cherokee Nation to document the blood quantum of Chief John Ross. Cherokee agent Hugh Montgomery replied with information on several of the leading men.[3] At this point the Cherokees were united in opposition to removal, and even when a faction defected, blood quantum played no role. Gilmer, however, wanted evidence to support his claim that the Nation was ruled by a clique of mixed-blood, mostly white, self-serving aristocrats who browbeat the full-blood "real"

Cherokees into opposing removal when they knew that it was in their best interest to go.

Resisting such persecution peaceably could not have been easy, even though all Cherokees knew that to fight back was dangerous. The General Council decided to do so, however, early in 1830, since their U.S. agent refused to do so. In 1829, Governor Gilmer decided that the final treaty with the Creeks, signed in 1827, had ceded to the state about one million acres that the Cherokee Nation claimed as part of its territory. Gilmer made his conclusion widely known, and hundreds of Georgians entered the disputed region, adjacent to Carroll County. Failing to gain the protection of the United States, the Council decided to exercise a right recognized in the 1791 Treaty of Holston to punish any Americans who crossed the line into their country illegally. Fearful of the reaction, the Cherokee Nation had never ejected intruders before. But one group of about twenty families, members of a gang of horse thieves called the Pony Club, had squatted along the main road to Alabama, and the Council was afraid that the Cherokees would be blamed for their crimes. The Council appointed Major Ridge, a prominent figure with a distinguished record as war leader and public servant, to lead a troop of Light Horse, the national police force, to evict the intruders. They did so, burning out the families, who later testified that they were terrified by Ridge, who wore a buffalo skull headdress complete with horns, and his men, painted for war. A posse from Carroll County tracked the Cherokee Light Horse and captured four, one of whom they beat to death. The others they carried off to jail. On the way, two escaped, but the third, Rattling Gourd, they held. Hugh Montgomery, the federal agent assigned to the Cherokee Nation, got him released with the argument that he was not an officer in the Light Horse, made no decisions, and was simply following orders. The central question, the right of the sheriff of Carroll County, Georgia, to enter the Cherokee Nation and arrest four Cherokees (not to mention killing one of them) for acting in accordance with a treaty provision, remained unanswered.[4]

Intrusion into the Cherokee Nation became further complicated with the discovery of gold on its land in 1829. Several thousand prospectors joined the Cherokees panning the streams, chased the Indians away, and then fell to fighting among themselves for choice sites. One source estimated that the miners took out some two thousand dollars of gold a day, wealth that would have had a dramatic impact on the Nation and its people. Again the United States did nothing to defend either the boundaries or the property rights of the Cherokees. Ultimately, Georgia forbade all mining, by Cherokees and non-Indians, on the theory that continued mining would cheat the "fortunate drawers" who won gold claims in the lottery.

The policy of Chief Ross and the Cherokee government in response to these provocations had three parts. One was a public-relations campaign. Friends of the Cherokees had been very active during the debate over the removal bill in 1829–30, and the American Board and other influential

Christian groups and individuals maintained a lively interest in the affairs of the Cherokees. John Ridge, David Vann, and Elias Boudinot, attractive, well-educated, and articulate young Cherokee men, made periodic lecture tours of eastern cities, where they often spoke to packed houses. But the *Cherokee Phoenix* was the centerpiece of the Nation's effort to keep the story of its rights and sufferings before the public. The National Council had authorized the establishment of a national newspaper in 1825. Funded through the Nation's treasury, the *Phoenix* began publication on February 21, 1828, with two clear purposes: to keep the Cherokee people informed on public issues and to demonstrate to the outside world the extent of Cherokee "civilization." Under the editorial direction of Elias Boudinot, the paper published the laws of the Nation, covered national political affairs, and ran stories on Cherokee culture and history. Much of this material appeared in parallel columns in English and Cherokee, using the syllabary invented by Sequoyah earlier in the decade and readable by a large percentage of Cherokees. Boudinot also published news from the United States and the world. The *Phoenix* had readers all over the United States and abroad, and Boudinot had exchange relations with over one hundred newspapers, many of which reprinted his editorials and other Cherokee news. Most Americans found it remarkable, some even unbelievable, that an Indian tribe produced a newspaper, and it therefore generated a great deal of public interest. Boudinot was a skillful editor and made the *Phoenix* an extraordinarily effective propaganda tool. "The wide circulation of the Cherokee Phoenix throughout the United States, have had a very salutary & happy effect," Ross announced to the General Council in 1831, "by enlightening the great mass of the people of the United States upon the Indian Cause."[5]

The second tactic of Chief Ross and the Cherokee government in response to Georgia's persecution was to lobby in Washington, presenting oral and written arguments, petitions, and memorials citing the history of their treaty relations, quoting the relevant treaty provisions and federal laws, and respectfully demanding that something be done to protect them from the escalating disruption of their social and economic well-being. The Cherokee delegations, at least one a year, sometimes two or three, traveled to Washington and made their case. The president, the officer required by the Constitution to enforce the laws of government, was their primary target, but his standard reply was that he had no power to override the sovereignty of Georgia, regardless of the treaties, and, therefore, if the Cherokees did not wish to live under the law of the state, they must sell out and emigrate. Though he sympathized with them and regretted their suffering, he professed, his hands were tied by the Constitution. It did not take long for the Cherokees to realize that Jackson and his administration welcomed, indeed encouraged, Georgia's harassment. The states could do the dirty work that drove the tribes to the treaty table, leaving Jackson free to pose as their protector. The Cherokees also lobbied Congress, although with less hope, understanding that additional legislation, if not enforced, was of little use.

The third tactic took the Cherokees into the courts. On June 3, 1830, six days after Jackson signed the Removal Act into law, the Georgia legislation that extended its jurisdiction into the Cherokee Nation went into effect. Getting hauled into Georgia courts was not unprecedented for the Cherokees, but neither was it common, and the General Council did not have a national policy on the problem. The threat, however, was clear. Many Cherokees would be arrested for violating Georgia law, and because they could not testify in their own defense, they would need legal representation. The Council, at Ross's request, authorized the chief to draw money from the treasury to hire attorneys, and Ross found several willing to serve Cherokee clients. At the same time, Ross and Jeremiah Evarts of the American Board had been corresponding about developing a federal case against Georgia's assertion of sovereign jurisdiction over the Nation. Evarts had suggested several names, including Massachusetts senator Daniel Webster, an attorney of legendary national reputation, but Webster suggested that they approach William Wirt of Baltimore. Wirt was one of the stars of the legal profession. He had been attorney general in the administrations of James Monroe and John Quincy Adams, and he was well known as a political enemy of Andrew Jackson. Although his decisions on Indian policy and tribal rights had been inconsistent, he was clearly no friend of the emergent doctrine of state sovereignty. With some skepticism, he agreed to do the preliminary research necessary to decide if the Cherokees could win their argument.

Through the summer of 1830 and in constant correspondence with Ross, Webster, Evarts, and other advisers, Wirt worked on the case. His brief, which Ross ordered published and distributed by the *Phoenix*, concluded that the legislation extending Georgia's civil and criminal jurisdiction over the Cherokee Nation was unconstitutional. Following a line of reasoning similar to the William Penn essays of Evarts, Wirt concluded that the law was repugnant to the treaties between the United States and the Cherokee Nation, Congress's 1802 Trade and Intercourse Act, and the commerce clause of the U.S. Constitution. Wirt was uncertain, however, about how to proceed. The easiest route was to appeal a case from a Georgia court, but Wirt did not relish dealing with that state's judiciary. An obvious tactic was to go directly to the U.S. Supreme Court seeking an injunction against the state, but jurisdiction was a problem. The U.S. Constitution gave the Supreme Court original jurisdiction in suits between the states and foreign nations, but Wirt was not convinced that the Cherokee Nation was a foreign nation. While he was trying to decide, in the fall of 1830 the sheriff of Hall County arrested a Cherokee man, Corn (or George) Tassel, for murder, charging him with killing another Cherokee man. The act occurred within the Cherokee Nation, thus presenting Wirt with a case challenging Georgia's jurisdiction. Judge Augustin S. Clayton heard the preliminaries in his Hall County court but deferred the trial until a tribunal of appellate judges ruled on the constitutionality of the extension legislation. William H. Underwood, a Georgia attorney Ross had hired to represent Tassel, presented the same treaty-based argument that the laws were unconstitutional. The state replied that the Cherokee Nation had neither national nor property rights, that the Compact of 1802 trumped the treaties, and that the commerce clause of the federal Constitution gave the United States authority only over trade relations. Thus the General Assembly had acted within its rights to extend the legal and political jurisdiction of the state over the Cherokee Nation, the sheriff acted properly to arrest Tassel for murder, and Judge Clayton's court had jurisdiction to try him. The judges agreed with the state's argument, Tassel's trial in Hall County resulted in conviction, and Judge Clayton sentenced him to hang on December 24. Wirt immediately appealed Tassel's conviction to the U.S. Supreme Court and asked the justices to overturn the verdict and block the execution. Chief Justice John Marshall granted Wirt's request and issued a subpoena requiring that Georgia governor George Gilmer appear before the bench in January. Gilmer called a special session of the legislature, and together they decided to ignore the subpoena and proceed with the hanging. Early on the morning of December 24, 1830, Hall County officials loaded a coffin into an oxcart, stood Tassel on the coffin under a tree at the end of a state rope, and drove the cart out from underneath him. Boudinot editorialized in the *Phoenix* that Georgia had "hoist[ed] the flag of rebellion against the United States," and if the government tolerated it, "the Union is but a tottering fabric, which will soon fall and crumble into atoms."[6] On December 27, 1830, three days after the Georgia court killed Tassel, Wirt filed before the Supreme Court the case that became *Cherokee Nation* v. *Georgia*.

In this, the first of the two landmark Cherokee cases decided by the Marshall Court in the early 1830s, Wirt based his presentation of the case on the claim that the Cherokee Nation met the constitutional conception of a foreign nation. The Nation, therefore, had standing before the Court and could argue for an injunction against the state of Georgia. Wirt and his cocounsel, John Sergeant, based their argument on the treaty history of the Cherokee Nation. The Cherokee Nation, they contended, retained sovereignty in all things except the two explicitly surrendered by treaty: The Nation agreed to sell land only to the United States, and it accepted U.S. control over its foreign relations and trade. Included in this assertion of retained sovereignty was the right to govern itself as a separate and distinct nation. Rejecting the right of discovery that Georgia claimed it inherited from England, the Nation also retained full authority over the land within its borders, and those rights both predated and were superior to Georgia's pretensions. By enacting and signing the law in question, Georgia's General Assembly and governor had unlawfully violated the sovereignty of the Cherokee Nation. The attorneys then described the effects of Georgia's illegal actions, including the trial and execution of Tassel, the imprisonment of several other Cherokees, and numerous infringements on their individual property rights. The Removal Act did not require emigration, reminded the attorneys, but the effect of Georgia's legislation, coupled with the refusal of the president to fulfill his constitutional obligation to execute the laws and treaties of the United States by protecting the sovereign rights of the Cherokee Nation, was tantamount to forcible expulsion. The argument lasted for three days in mid-March 1831. Georgia, denying any jurisdiction of the Supreme Court in state affairs, refused to appear.

Six justices heard the case, and their split decision amounts to a 2-2-2 vote. Two justices concluded that the Cherokee Nation was neither a foreign state nor a sovereign nation and that Cherokee individuals were subjects of the state of Georgia. Two argued that the Cherokee Nation was sovereign, had standing before the Court as a foreign state, and was entitled to protection against the unconstitutional laws of Georgia. And two, including Chief Justice John Marshall, decided between the two extremes. The Cherokee Nation lacked standing because it was not a foreign state, but it deserved to be recognized and respected, although as what was not altogether clear, despite Marshall's efforts to describe it. At any rate, four justices agreed to deny the Cherokee Nation standing. Chief Justice Marshall wrote the opinion that the Cherokee Nation could not sue the state of Georgia, and the Court threw out the case for lack of jurisdiction. The justices did not address the Cherokee claim that the legislation of Georgia was unconstitutional and should be declared null and void.

The crucial question in the case was whether the Cherokee Nation was a foreign state. Marshall accepted Wirt's contention that it was "a distinct political society, separated from others, capable of managing its own affairs and governing itself." The Cherokee Nation was a state and had been "uniformly treated as a state from the settlement of the country."

The treaties verified such a conclusion, and Congress had enacted laws accordingly. "The acts of our government plainly recognize the Cherokee nation as a state, and the Courts are bound by those acts." But in Marshall's view the Cherokee state was not a foreign one. The problem was that the tribes were within the boundaries of the United States, they had accepted the protection of the United States in the treaties, and they had agreed that the United States had the exclusive right to manage their trade. And while they had rights to the land, they "occupy a territory to which we assert a title independent of their will, which must take effect in point of possession when their right of possession ceases." All this denied their foreignness. Searching for an acceptable definition, Marshall coined the term "domestic dependent nation," which he tried to explain by analogy. The tribes were in a "state of pupilage," he wrote, and had a relationship with the United States that "resembles that of a ward to his guardian."[7] Several members of a Cherokee delegation, described by observers as "intelligent and respectful," sat in the gallery during the case, reportedly crying when Wirt recited the troubles Georgia forced their people to endure. They returned home in April 1831, ready to report.

The Cherokee people were well aware of the suit and were eager for the salvation it promised. Chief Ross tried to put the best face on the decision by telling the General Council that it was a victory because the Court recognized that they were "a distinct political society, separated from others, capable of managing its own affairs and governing itself."

This, Ross announced, was "conclusively adverse" to Georgia's claims and, on balance, was more important than the loss of the injunction. Furthermore, Ross stressed his view that, if the Nation could come up with a case that satisfied the Court's jurisdictional requirements, it was sure to win: "Our cause will ultimately triumph."[8] Editor Boudinot was not so certain. He rejoiced that the Court "explicitly acknowledged and conceded" the rights of the Cherokee Nation, but "we are at the same time considered to be in a state of 'pupilage,' unable to sue for those rights in the judicial tribunals. This is certainly no enviable position."[9] Boudinot was more right than Ross. Marshall's definition of the tribes as "domestic dependent nations" in a relationship with the United States that resembled that between a ward and guardian has become, in the 175 years since the decision, a powerful tool for those who seek to inhibit the efforts of Native nations to exercise sovereignty.

During the winter of 1830–31, while the *Cherokee Nation* case was pending, the Georgia legislature forged ahead with a new battery of laws designed to exercise the jurisdiction it claimed over the part of the Cherokee Nation within its boundaries. The first priority was to divide the country into land districts and establish the procedure for its survey and distribution by lottery. The law also extended the service of the Georgia Guard to protect the surveyors from harassment by Cherokees and provided punishments for any person who interfered with the survey. The legislature voted to defer the survey one year, however, in case the Cherokee Nation and the United States concluded a removal treaty. In December 1831, in the absence of the desired treaty, the legislature authorized the governor to begin the survey in April 1832 and commence the lottery as soon as the survey was complete. The lawmakers included in the survey law a provision to prohibit fortunate drawers in the lottery from evicting Cherokees who owned improvements on the lots they drew. In such cases only, Cherokees could testify against whites in court. Another act authorized the governor to "take possession" of the gold district and station a Guard force there to keep the peace and oust trespassers. The result was that the disposition of the entire region was fully in the hands of the state of Georgia.

The legislation enacted by the Georgia Assembly in December 1830 also provided that any "white person" living in the Cherokee Nation after March 1, 1831, who had not taken an oath promising loyal obedience to the laws of Georgia and received a special permit from the governor was liable to prosecution and imprisonment for not less than four years at hard labor. Only white men married to Cherokee women and "authorized agents" of the U.S. government were exempted. Everyone knew that the law targeted the missionaries, outsiders widely believed to be active advisers against removal. A few missionaries took the oath, and some relocated across the line into Tennessee, but several American Board missionaries chose to do neither. They would test the law, and if arrested, convicted, and sentenced, they would provide Wirt with a case on appeal that the Supreme Court would accept.

On March 12, 1831, the Georgia Guard arrested the missionaries and hauled them into court, where William Underwood, the attorney working for the Cherokee Nation, defended them on the grounds that Georgia's laws had no jurisdiction over them because the Cherokee Nation was sovereign. Augustin Clayton, the judge who had ordered the hanging of Tassel only a few weeks before, figured that the missionaries were planning a test case and released them. All the mission organizations received subsidies from the federal government, and Reverend Samuel Worcester was U.S. postmaster at New Echota. These facts, Clayton decided, qualified them as federal agents. A quick letter to the secretary of war removed that worry, and the postmaster general fired Worcester. When the good news reached Governor Gilmer, he ordered them arrested once again. On July 7, the Guard took Worcester, Doctor Elizur Butler, and nine other missionaries to Gwinnett County, harassing and mistreating them all the way. The Guard chained Butler by the neck to their wagon and made him walk the entire eighty-five miles. Judge Clayton heard their case in mid-September, the arguments once again hanging on the question of Georgia's jurisdiction. After a deliberation of fifteen minutes, the jury found them guilty. Governor Gilmer, fearing the bad national press if the state threw all these churchmen in jail, hoped the missionaries would either take the oath or leave the state. Nine accepted Gilmer's offer, Worcester and Butler refused, and the Cherokees and Wirt had their case.

Wirt filed an appeal, the Supreme Court issued a sub poena, and Wilson Lumpkin, the newly elected governor of Georgia, was as adamant in his refusal to recognize the authority of the Court over the actions of his state as his predecessor, George Gilmer, had been. In November 1831, when the order to appear before the Court reached his desk, Lumpkin sent it to the General Assembly, which directed him to ignore it. In a replay of the *Cherokee Nation* hearing the year before, no Georgian appeared to rebut Wirt's presentation. The hearing commenced February 20, 1832. Wirt and Sergeant largely repeated the arguments in favor of the sovereignty of the Cherokee Nation that they had developed in the *Cherokee Nation* case, but in important ways the situation was very different. The year 1832 was an election year, and Jackson was eager for the voters' endorsement of his policies. Both Wirt and Sergeant were on opposing presidential tickets—Sergeant as the National Republicans' vice presidential candidate with Henry Clay at the top of the ticket and Wirt as the presidential nominee of the Anti-Masonic Party. The case thus had political implications beyond the interests of the missionaries, Georgia, or the Cherokee Nation. Congressmen, senators, and the press packed the courtroom in the basement of the Capitol.

It was an open secret that Chief Justice Marshall was sympathetic to the Cherokees and believed that Georgia's legislation was both unjust and unconstitutional. Nevertheless, the two attorneys took three days to make their case. Chief

Justice Marshall issued the 6–1 decision on March 3. The law Samuel A. Worcester was convicted of violating, the Court found, was "void, as repugnant to the Constitution, treaties, and laws of the United States," and the conviction should be "reversed and annulled."[10] The lasting significance of this decision is less in its final judgment, however, than in the body of Marshall's opinion.

After Marshall addressed the question of jurisdiction, which was never in dispute, he wrote a long and careful analysis of the history of the relations between the Cherokee Nation and England and then with the United States. England had treated the tribes as sovereign and negotiated treaties of alliance with them. The United States followed suit, thus continuing the practice of recognizing tribal sovereignty. When the United States assumed the role of protector of the tribes, it neither denied nor destroyed their sovereignty. Instead, such a relationship both preserved tribal government and protected it from the states. As a result of their relations with the United States, tribal sovereignty had been diminished in specific ways, but in all other things the tribes retained the sovereignty that had been theirs since time immemorial. Furthermore, only the United States could deal with the Cherokee Nation, because treaty relations are government-to-government relations, the unique concern of sovereign states. "The Cherokee nation," Marshall concluded, "is a distinct community, occupying its own territory, with boundaries accurately described, in which the laws of Georgia can have no force."[11] In striking down the Georgia legislation, Marshall asserted that the federal government had supreme authority in conducting relations with Native nations. Useful in protecting the tribes from state encroachment, this idea of federal plenary power has been a double-edged sword, which has also been used to hack away at tribal sovereignty. But the idea that tribes retain all those attributes of sovereignty not explicitly surrendered or denied by Congress has been a significant source of power upon which tribes continue to rely.[12]

The *Worcester* v. *Georgia* decision gratified Chief Ross. Not only had the Court affirmed the sovereignty of the Cherokee Nation, it had redirected the conflict into one between Georgia and the United States, which was an enormous relief. On the other hand, Ross was enough of a realist to be skeptical. The decision was a wonderful thing but without enforcement it changed nothing. Only time would tell.

In the Cherokee Nation, on the other hand, the decision of the Court had a "most powerful effect." In every community, it seemed, the people celebrated with "Rejoicings Dances and Meetings." As William Williamson, an officer in the Georgia Guard stationed in Cherokee country, reported to Governor Lumpkin, "They not only believed that the right of Jurisdiction was restored but that they were Sovereign independent nation & the U. S. bound by Treaty to afford them protection."[13] Like Ross, Williamson was skeptical. But while Williamson belittled the idea of Cherokee sovereignty,

Ross championed it. Along with his "honest patriotism and love of country," it gave him strength and hope. He thanked William Wirt for his work on behalf of the Nation and promised to pay him, someday, but he knew that the fight was not over.

JOHN RIDGE,

A CHEROKEE.

PUBLISHED BY F. W. GREENOUGH PHILAD.A

John Ridge had a distinguished career as a Cherokee statesman, but he signed the removal treaty of 1835 and in 1839 paid for that act with his life. From Thomas L. McKenney and James Hall, History of the Indian Tribes of North America *(Philadelphia: F. W. Greenough, 1838–44); copy in the Rare Book Collections, Wilson Library, University of North Carolina, Chapel Hill.*

5

THE TREATY OF NEW ECHOTA

❦

"IF ONE HUNDRED PERSONS are ignorant of their true situation, and are so completely blinded as not to see the destruction that awaits them," Elias Boudinot wrote in 1837, "we can see strong reasons to justify the action of a minority of fifty persons to do what the majority *would do* if they understood their condition—to save a *nation* from political thralldom and moral degradation."[1] Boudinot and his associates, members of the so-called "treaty party," repeated this explanation many times to justify their actions in concluding the Treaty of New Echota, which provided for removal, in late December 1835. Their love of their nation, they cried, made their deed right and would, they hoped, exonerate them in the end. What the fate of the Cherokees might have been had there been no negotiation at New Echota is impossible to tell, of course, but to Boudinot, his uncle Major Ridge, his cousin John Ridge, his brother Stand Watie, and a handful of others, it would have been a fate worse than removal.[2]

The Removal Act of 1830 left many things unspecified, including the means by which the removal of the eastern Indian nations to the country set aside for them west of the Mississippi would be arranged. The reason for this apparent vagueness, however, is clear. Every Trade and Intercourse Act passed by Congress, from the first in 1790 to the last in 1834, stipulated that all sales of land by tribes to the United States must be accomplished by treaty. The treaty system, well established by the 1830s, rested on the supposition that the treaties were contracts between sovereigns equally empowered to agree or disagree with the proposals on the table. Through negotiation they reached a mutually satisfactory arrangement, and by signing and ratifying the document, they obligated themselves to fulfill its terms. Voluntarism was the guiding principle of treaty making. Unless it was a peace treaty at the end of a war, neither side could force the other to negotiate. The government of Andrew Jackson could demand that the Cherokee Nation discuss the terms of a removal treaty, but if the Nation's leaders refused to talk or, after talking, refused to agree, there was nothing legal the president could do. That is why the actions of Georgia are so important to the history of the removal of the Cherokees. That state, with the connivance of the president, intended to make life for the Cherokees so miserable they would decide that emigration was salvation and eagerly sign any treaty presented to them just to get away. The Cherokee Nation also reached into Alabama, Tennessee, and North Carolina. Alabama extended its jurisdiction the year after Georgia, and Tennessee did so in 1835. Because they were public land states and title reverted to the federal not the state government, Alabama and Tennessee did not gain immediate control of land sold by the tribe as Georgia did. As a result, their policies were much less aggressive than Georgia's.

Georgia's legislation could not have pleased President Andrew Jackson more if he had written the laws himself. The Cherokees, however, knew that influential people disagreed with Jackson and supported the claims to sovereignty by the Cherokee Nation. Men from the religious establishment like Jeremiah Evarts and Theodore Frelinghuysen, the "Christian Senator," had based their opposition to the removal act on their belief in the sovereignty of the Cherokee Nation. Their arguments, along with partisan opponents of Jackson and the Democratic Party, had nearly defeated the act in the House of Representatives. Following its passage, Chief Ross worked tirelessly to cultivate these men. They advised him on a legal strategy and helped him identify William Wirt to present the Cherokee case before the Supreme Court. Furthermore, Evarts's American Board conspired with its missionaries in the Cherokee Nation to defy Georgia law by refusing to take the prescribed oath of allegiance to the state, thereby sacrificing themselves in order to make a test case that the Supreme Court would accept. John Ridge and Elias Boudinot were in the Boston office of the American Board when they received news of the Court's decision in the *Worcester* case. The two Cherokees and their ministerial hosts jumped to their feet, hugged one another, and danced a jig around Evarts's desk in jubilation. These were the kinds of friends that the Cherokees could count on, it seemed.

Ridge and Boudinot immediately returned to Washington to join the other members of the Cherokee delegation. When they arrived, the celebration was already over. Ridge wrote his cousin Stand Watie that he felt "greatly revived—a new man" and "independent," but he knew that the "contest is not over. . . . The Chicken Snake General Jackson has time to crawl and hide in the luxuriant grass of his nefarious hypocracy."[3] The word was out that their victory in Court was hollow. Jackson affirmed the rumor in a private audience with Ridge—he would not act to execute the Court's decision in *Worcester*. Fearful of a constitutional crisis, congressional friends and confidants of the Cherokees took members of the delegation aside to recommend that they give up. Justice John McLean, a better friend on the Court than Chief Justice Marshall, advised them that there was nothing more they could do to resist removal. Sell now and get the best deal you can, he urged. He even volunteered to serve as a U.S. commissioner and negotiate the treaty himself. Then, in early May 1832, Ridge got word from the American Board that the missionaries wanted them to emigrate. By the end of the year, Worcester and Butler, serving hard time in the Georgia penitentiary, had asked for and received gubernatorial pardons. Agreeing to leave the state, they gave up all plans to pursue their cases any further. The South Carolina nullification crisis was afoot, though the issue was the tariff, not Indians. Nevertheless, politicians in both parties feared that Georgia, which actually was engaged in nullifying federal law, might join its neighbor state and exacerbate the threat of disunion if it felt pressured by the Supreme Court. So everybody, friends as well as enemies, sacrificed the Cherokees.

Taking advantage of their anguish, Secretary of War Lewis Cass called the Cherokee delegates to his office in mid-April 1832 and outlined the terms of a treaty. His gall disgusted Ridge. How can we trust "an administration who have trampled our rights under foot to offer new pledges from their rotten hearts," he asked.[4] But the details differed from the other removal treaties negotiated by the Jackson administration over the previous two years, and in some ways, they were surprisingly generous. The western land the Cherokees would receive in exchange for all their holdings in the East would be surveyed and conveyed to the Nation by patent, which meant that it would be legally theirs and not subject to later charges that they were occupants and users but not owners. The United States would protect the Cherokees from non-Indian intruders and attacks from western Indians, subsist them on their new lands during their first year, and build and support schools, provide blacksmiths and iron, and construct churches, public buildings, and even homes for the most important chiefs. The United States also would guarantee to the Nation its right to self-government and authorize it to send to Washington both an agent (lobbyist) to look after its affairs and a delegate to Congress. In addition to the exchange of land, the United States would pay into the Cherokee treasury the value of the eastern cession plus all other annuities owed the Nation. To individuals, the government would pay compensation for their personal property and livestock left behind plus supply all sorts of gear, such as rifles, blankets, tools, and implements, calculated to be useful in Indian Territory.

The delegates listened carefully. Some already had lost heart. President Jackson, in describing his conversation with John Ridge, observed that he had "expressed despair," and Amos Kendall, one of Jackson's closest advisers, recalled that "Ridge left the President with the melancholy feeling that he had [heard] the truth."[5] Elias Boudinot shared his cousin's "despair," and others of the delegation, including John Martin and William Shorey Coodey, were dejected. But they had not been empowered by the General Council of the Nation to travel to Washington to negotiate a treaty, and they informed Cass that they would not carry it back with them. Cass put the terms proposed into the hands of Elisha Chester, one of the attorneys working for the Nation, and together they headed home to report.

The Cherokee capital, New Echota, lay within Georgia's boundaries, but because Georgia law criminalized all governmental activity by Cherokees, the councilors had decided in the summer of 1831 to move their deliberations for that fall to Chatooga, a site across the line in Alabama that had been developed for religious camp meetings. Chatooga was far from the center of Cherokee population and thus inconvenient, so beginning in 1832 the Council moved to Red Clay in the Tennessee part of the Nation. Two important things happened there when the delegates returned. One was that the Council overruled John Ross and decided to hear from Chester the terms Cass had suggested. In the name of unity and to avoid confusing the people, Ross had tried to prevent public discussion of a treaty. Second, the councilors voted to suspend elections, declaring themselves and Chief Ross legitimate until such time as the Nation's government was not under Georgia's proscription. Ridge and Boudinot opposed Ross's efforts to suppress discussion of the terms of the treaty and applauded the decision of the Council to explore every option. But they did not like the decision to suspend elections. Ridge harbored political ambitions. He already served on the National Committee, but he believed he was better qualified than Ross to sit as principal chief. He had intended to oppose Ross in the fall elections and resented being denied the opportunity to run. It is impossible to say how much this resentment figured into his future actions, but by the middle of 1832, John Ridge was disgusted with the leadership of John Ross and had developed an agenda of his own, the central feature of which was to sell out on the best terms available and get the Cherokee people as far away as possible from Georgia. Boudinot agreed with his cousin, and on their return to the Nation, they discovered that Major Ridge, who recently had made an extensive and shocking tour of the Nation, had reached a similar conclusion. Boudinot's brother,

Stand Watie, and a handful of others, joined them. Together they struggled to present an alternative to the policy of the principal chief.

Ross's strategy was first to encourage the Cherokee people in their universal opposition to removal. In speaking tours and in his annual messages to the General Council every October, Chief Ross reminded the Nation of the justice and righteousness of the cause of the Cherokees and pledged that the goodwill of the American people and the institutions of American government would ultimately join in the affirmation of Cherokee national sovereignty. They had the treaties and the Trade and Intercourse Acts on their side, and since the *Worcester* decision they had the Supreme Court as well. But Ross knew that faith and hope was a fragile message, and he worked to strengthen it by suppressing all contrary opinions. Divergent views simply confused the people, he believed, and potentially led to disunity and weakened resolve. To this end, he opposed Boudinot's wishes to use the *Cherokee Phoenix* as a forum for debating policy alternatives. Bristling at such censorship and charging that Ross was attempting to deny the people the information necessary to make intelligent decisions, Boudinot resigned as editor of the paper in August 1832.

Consistent with his faith in the people and institutions of the United States, Ross's strategy also combined public relations and political manipulation. The large anti-Jackson press eagerly publicized the suffering of the Cherokees at the hands of Georgia and the president. Petitions delivered to the

War Department and the White House by Cherokee delegates and the voluminous correspondence between them and federal officials filled thousands of newspaper pages. Memorials presented to the House and Senate by sympathetic politicians supplemented this material, generated debate in Congress that fed Ross's hopes for legislative relief, and wound up published and disseminated in the many volumes of House and Senate documents. The sameness of the arguments, the logic, the examples, and the citations year after year as one failed petition followed another is remarkable. Partly, Ross was stalling. In the summer of 1832 he hoped Henry Clay and the new Whig Party would defeat Jackson. Then, assuming that Jackson would follow the precedent established by George Washington and retire after two terms, 1836 promised renewed hope. After Jackson, no one could be worse. Partly, though, Ross simply wanted to make certain that the American people could not forget the Cherokees. That, too, kept his hope alive. And, of course, he had almost boundless faith in the moral power of the Cherokee people and their cause. He simply could not give up.

Instead of a Clay victory, the summer of 1832 brought a horde of surveyors working under state law to lay out Cherokee Georgia into lots, each with a number that would go into the lottery wheel in the fall. By November, "fortunate drawers" had begun to swarm into the Nation to claim their winnings. This was theft authorized by state law, but theft nonetheless, of millions of acres of land. The General Assembly included in its legislation a provision that protected the right of Cherokee families to occupy the lots that held their farms, but Georgia authorities were not enthusiastic about evicting Georgians who ignored the law and drove Cherokees out of their homes. One Georgia newspaper guessed that despite the guarantee promised by the legislature, by the end of 1835 about two-thirds of the Cherokees in the state were homeless. If the state could steal the undeveloped land of the Cherokees, why should the lottery winners not steal their homes?

Ross, of course, was helpless. Neither he nor the Cherokee government had authority in that part of the Nation claimed by Georgia. The Council hired attorneys periodically and managed to prosecute some of the worst offenders in the Georgia courts, but there were too many, and in any event, the Nation was broke and could not pay the legal fees. Since its first cession of land to the United States in 1791 the Cherokee Nation had received every year a stipend from Congress. Called annuities, the money was partial payment for the land. The Council established a treasury, the treasurer collected the money, and the Nation had cash to fund its activities. Beginning in 1830, about the time Ross hired William Wirt to represent the Nation in the Supreme Court, Jackson ordered that henceforth the annuity payment must be divided and paid per capita to each individual Cherokee. Jackson's rule was designed to deny the Cherokee Nation the funds needed to defend its rights, although he explained it by claiming that the leaders used the money for themselves and cheated the people of their fair share. Divided per capita, their fair share was forty-three cents, and they had to travel to the U.S. agency, for many a trip of one hundred miles or more, to get it. Almost none bothered, and for four years the annuity went into an escrow account that none of the Cherokee leaders could touch. On more than one occasion, Ross had to pass his hat to collect money to pay the lawyers.

To some, Ross's policy of presenting petitions, sending memorials and letters, and hoping for good news was useless. Perhaps it was worse than useless, because he refused to try a new policy. Ridge and his father, Boudinot and his brother, and a small but growing number of others became increasingly convinced that Ross's policy of faith and hope, public relations and petitioning, was leading nowhere. Ridge managed to gain the floor at the October 1832 meeting of the General Council and delivered an impassioned speech urging that the delegation about to leave for Washington be instructed to discuss treaty terms, but he failed to sway the Council. He refused, however, to abandon his efforts to convince Ross and the people to change their minds. In early February 1833 Ridge wrote Ross to warn him that a group of men were on their way to Washington to undercut the official delegation and talk about a removal treaty. Ridge did not approve of either the men or their decision to act without authority, but he reminded Ross that "other Gentlemen with myself [have] despaired of the existence of our dear nation upon its present Location" and urged him to listen to the advice of the Nation's friends in Washington. Our people are being "robbed & whipped by the whites almost every day," and Ross had to do something. "I know you are capable of acting the part of a statesman," Ridge wrote, and "we all know, upon consultation in Council, that we can't be a Nation here, I hope we shall attempt to establish it somewhere else!"[6] Jackson offered Ross $3 million for the lands of the Cherokees in the East and promised federal protection of the Nation's rights in the West. The chief refused. The sum was too small and, Ross snapped, why should we believe your promises of protection now?

Without federal protection from Georgia, the situation in the Cherokee Nation got progressively worse, and relations between Ridge and Ross worsened as well. Ross reacted to Ridge's critiques with charges of treason, and the atmosphere at the October 1833 meeting of the General Council was especially tense. In his annual message, however, Ross broached the question of removal for the first time and, in the process, hinted at an emergent frustration with the people and institutions of the United States. If it became necessary to emigrate, he announced, it should be "beyond the limits of the United States."[7] Some had suggested that the mouth of the Columbia River might be a good place. Ross may not have been serious but the idea remained in his mind.

Ross led the delegation to Washington later that fall. While he was away, in December 1833, the Georgia legislature gave the screw one more turn with a law that authorized "fortunate drawers" to occupy the improved property of those Cherokees who hired whites. It also declared that all contracts between an Indian and a white man were void unless witnessed by two "respectable" (non-Indian) witnesses. The Georgians claimed that the wealthy leaders of the Cherokee Nation were blocking the "common" Indians in their desire to remove because they did not want to surrender their plantations and businesses. Many of the big planters and entrepreneurs in the Nation, including Ross and his brothers, employed white men. Designed to impoverish the economic elite, the law convinced Ross's brother Andrew that the time had come to treat. At the head of a delegation that included Elias Boudinot and Major Ridge, Andrew Ross arrived in Washington so eager to settle things that he refused to negotiate and signed a humiliating deal. Appalled by the paltry terms, Boudinot and Ridge disassociated themselves, but fear of brother Andrew's arrangement drove Chief Ross to make the government an offer. He would sell most of the land in Georgia if the president would promise to protect the rights of the Nation to the rest of its territory for a specified period of years, at which time the Cherokees would become equal citizens of the states and abide by state law. The Cherokee Nation would cease to exist, and the Cherokee people would embrace their inevitable future of "amalgamation."[8] Major Ridge and Boudinot found Ross's idea that the future for the Cherokees was to become Americans equally appalling. To them, "amalgamation" was neither inevitable nor acceptable. To surrender the Cherokee people to Georgia racism would destroy them. Jackson rejected the chief's proposal and submitted Andrew Ross's treaty to the Senate for ratification. But the senators were also appalled and withheld their approval, citing the obvious fact that it had been negotiated with an unofficial delegation.[9]

When the national delegation returned home in the spring of 1834 to report on its activities in Washington, Ross did not disclose to the Council his offer to Jackson about citizenship and amalgamation. Instead, he played up Andrew's duplicitous actions and linked them to the arguments of the Ridges. People began to mutter threats against them, and Elijah Hicks, now editor of the *Cherokee Phoenix*, presented a petition of impeachment against John Ridge and David Vann, members of the National Committee, and Major Ridge, national councilor. Ross let the petition lie on the table in order to deny them a public forum, but he could not keep them entirely quiet. The Ridge party walked out of the Council grounds and called a rump council at John Ridge's plantation where they hammered out a position between the two proposals of John and Andrew Ross. They probably believed that time had run out. At the end of May, Georgia governor Wilson Lumpkin had written an open letter to Senator John Forsyth in which he predicted that "before the close of the year it may become necessary to remove every Cherokee from the limits of Georgia, peaceably if we can, forcibly if we must."[10] Forsyth publicized the letter and no doubt the Cherokees knew about it. The Ridge council appointed a delegation, including John Ridge and Boudinot, to challenge the delegates led to Washington by Ross.

At the same time, Lumpkin arranged with the state's authorities in Cherokee Georgia to make sure that no "fortunate drawers" laid claim to the homes of Ridge, Boudinot, or any of their friends. Eager to give them all the encouragement he could, he no doubt also wanted it known in the Nation that Cherokees who joined their movement would be safe from dispossession by Georgians. Cherokees of property who opposed a treaty could expect the opposite. A "fortunate drawer" had already laid claim to Ross's home, but the chief hired an attorney and got him evicted. The next time it happened, early in 1835 while Ross was in Washington, he lost. Having been gone for several months, the chief rode up to his house to find a strange Georgia family sitting at his dinner table. It was too late to press on so he rented a room for the night, and the next morning he found his wife and family in a two-room cabin across the line in Tennessee.

The two delegations competed for attention in Washington. Both submitted memorials to Congress. The Ridge delegation blasted the administration for refusing to respect the sovereignty of the Cherokee Nation and permitting Georgia to rob them of their land, thus forcing them to the treaty table. The national delegation renewed Ross's amalgamation plan. The Cherokee Nation would cede all of their land in Georgia except for a tiny strip, so worthless that no "fortunate drawers" would want it, to connect their lands in Alabama, Tennessee, and North Carolina. The Cherokees would receive fee simple title for this country, the United States would purchase the claims of Georgia lottery winners, the states would organize the region into counties, and the people would become fully equal citizens of the states. More extreme than his proposal of the year before, in a later period this plan would be called allotment and termination. The

Ridge party rejected it because it would obliterate the Cherokee Nation and subject the people to the racist discrimination
of the states. The president rejected it because he would accept nothing short of removal to the West. And Georgia governor Lumpkin became apoplectic when he learned of the
proposal. Jackson then turned to the Ridge party and appointed John F. Schermerhorn, a retired Dutch Reformed
minister from New York, to negotiate terms. In the midst of
those talks, Ross came back with a final offer. For $20 mil-
lion he would sell everything and sever all ties with the
United States. The payment would cover the land, the private improvements and possessions of the people, and the
cost of emigration. In addition, the United States would pay
compensation for damages caused by the illegal actions of the
neighboring states and their citizens and fulfill earlier treaty
obligations to provide school funds and pay annuities. The
United States would also have to protect the personal and
property rights of the Cherokees for five years or until they
had moved out. Ross said nothing about where the Cherokees
would go, but in secret he opened correspondence with Mexi-
can authorities about the possibility of creating an Indian state
in Mexico. Jackson ridiculed the figure, claiming the Senate
would never ratify such an arrangement, so Ross agreed to let
the Senate name a number. It came back with $5 million, the
sum the Ridges and Schermerhorn had tentatively agreed on,
which Ross argued was far too low. In light of over $6 million
worth of coins ultimately minted from Cherokee gold, the
United States stood to make a tidy profit on the deal.[11]

Back in the Cherokee Nation, early in the summer of 1835, Ross reported no headway in Washington and urged the General Council to reject the draft prepared by the Ridge delegation and Schermerhorn. But a cloud of fear hung over the Nation. Governor Lumpkin had broadcast his opinion that the Cherokees should be treated like orphan children incapable of making decisions, and instead of continuing to fool around negotiating a removal agreement, the government, either his or Jackson's, should simply legislate their expulsion.[12] The Ridges called a series of open meetings to explain the terms they had negotiated. While at first few people attended, at successive gatherings the numbers grew into the thousands. Fearful of losing control, Ross suggested that a group of men from his camp meet in private with a group from Ridge's camp and together perhaps they could reach an agreement that would reunify the Nation. The Ridges, always hopeful that Ross would embrace their thinking, agreed. The two groups argued in private for five days and emerged with expressions of goodwill and national harmony and a resolution to Congress that both sides could sign. The plan was to send another delegation to Washington, but Jackson wanted the treaty, if there was to be one, signed in the Cherokee Nation. He did not want another delegation visiting him. The Cherokees sent a delegation anyway, one that included John Ridge and others of his party. Schermerhorn, who had been in the Nation politicking for a treaty since spring, obeyed his orders and called for a meeting at New Echota in December.

The delegation to Washington got off to an inauspicious start. Elias Boudinot resigned his appointment before it left, and shortly thereafter, at Athens, Tennessee, John Ridge threatened to quit and return home. He had read a piece by John Howard Payne, a poet and the author of "Home, Sweet Home" who had come into the Nation some months before to gather information for a series of articles, that said that the Cherokees would prefer to remain in the East as citizens of the states rather than to remove to the West. Assuming that this remained Ross's position, Ridge interpreted Payne's article as a violation of the agreement the two parties had made in November. No doubt remembering his experience at Cornwall, Ridge wrote that because he and his friends "will never consent to be citizens of the United States," he could no longer cooperate with the chief.[13] Only after Ross claimed that that was not his current position and pleaded with him to remain a member of the delegation did Ridge consent to proceed.

If anything, things were worse in the Cherokee Nation. Governor Lumpkin's term ended in November, and he was depressed that there would be no removal treaty with the Cherokee Nation before his retirement. He so believed that getting rid of the Cherokees was his mission in life that he entitled his autobiography, written some twenty years later, *The Removal of the Cherokees from Georgia*. He was proud that he had come so close, however, and decided that with his valedictory act he could fulfill his dream. In letters calculated to be widely discussed in the Cherokee Nation, he mused that a treaty really was not necessary. The General Assembly had already accomplished more in four years than the United States had achieved in thirty, and all it would take was one more piece of legislation. He would be out of office before it was enacted, but he could recommend it in his last annual message, and he did.[14] On December 21, 1835, about the time the delegation set out for Washington and the day before the council called by Schermerhorn met at New Echota, the Georgia Assembly did his bidding and legislated the Cherokees out of the state with a law that authorized all "fortunate drawers" of lots occupied by Cherokees to take possession of their winnings on November 25, 1836. Cherokees who had managed to hang on until then could expect some Georgian to come along and throw them out of their houses, and there would be nothing at all that they could do about it. Once homeless, Lumpkin assumed, the Cherokees would have to leave.

No one, Indian or American, was in doubt about the purposes of this legislation. The obvious and stated intent of the General Assembly of Georgia was to put its citizens into possession of the land owned by the Cherokee Nation. A purpose equally obvious, if not stated, was to drive the Cherokees to the treaty table and out of the state. In a long preamble to the short act, they repeated the old saw that Indians were "savages" who, when brought into "contact with civilized man . . . rapidly sink into a corresponding state of degradation." In order to protect them from such a fate, "the past policy of the State, in relation to this tribe of Indians, should be carried out, to wit, securing to these aborigines a distant establishment." This would require the repeal of previous legislation that denied "fortunate drawers" possession of lots on which Cherokees lived. If "the right of occupancy of the lands in their possession should be withdrawn, . . . it would be a strong inducement to them to treat with the general government and consent to a removal to the west." The legislature originally gave the Cherokees eleven months to get ready, but following the ratification of the Treaty of New Echota, the General Assembly extended the date of dispossession to May 25, 1838.[15]

Half the Cherokees did not live in Georgia and did not face this menace, but half did. Understandably, most of the Cherokees who followed the Ridges and Boudinot lived in that part of the Nation claimed by Georgia. The hard-line opposition of the General Council and Ross's policy of passive resistance and stalling did not meet the needs of the half that lived with the Georgians. Schermerhorn was smart to call his council to meet at New Echota. Located in the Georgia part of the Nation, it had not functioned as the national capital since 1830 and had ceased to be the logical place for such a meeting of all Cherokees. But Schermerhorn wanted a treaty, and he knew that the Cherokees most likely to show up would be those nearby who were hurting the most. He advertised the council widely with handbills printed in Cherokee, but he betrayed his expectation that few would attend by announcing that those who stayed away would be counted as favoring whatever transpired.

Including the women and children who accompanied their husbands and fathers, maybe five hundred people turned out to hear what Schermerhorn had to say. The number of men who voted was eighty-six. Schermerhorn, nicknamed the Devil's Horn by the Cherokees because he was a notorious womanizer, described the terms for the removal treaty he had discussed with the Ridge delegation the previous winter. While he was talking, the roof of the building caught fire, suggesting the "indignation of Heaven" to one antitreaty observer. Following his presentation, the Cherokees appointed a committee of twenty to consider the terms. After a few days of haggling, the council reconvened, and the committee reported that they had drafted a good treaty. On December 29, 1835, those present voted, and the twenty members of the negotiating committee signed their names to the document. Seventy-nine approved, seven opposed. The council then appointed a delegation to carry the document to Washington. Headed by Major Ridge and Boudinot, their first task was to sell it to Ross. They were not happy with what they had done. Their goal had always been to convert Ross to their point of view. They knew that the Cherokees did not want to remove; they did not want to move either. But they believed Ross could have persuaded the people of the necessity of removal if he had tried. This was what frustrated them. And while they hoped to convince him, they knew he would not join them now. Thus their secondary plan was to give the treaty to Jackson and follow his lead.

The official delegation had been in Washington for

many days when news arrived about the treaty. The delegates had met with Jackson and had been surprised by his apparent good humor, considering that they had come to the capital against his orders. But they had had no substantive talks, and the War Department refused to recognize the delegation as legitimate. The New Echota group arrived early in February, but Ross would have nothing to do with them. Instead he wrote home to ask Assistant Chief George Lowrey to organize a petition against the treaty. Lowrey sent over fourteen thousand names. At the same time, John Ridge and Stand Watie, members of the national delegation, moved over to the treaty group and added their names to the document.

The treaty signed at New Echota obligated the Cherokees to surrender all their lands in the East and remove to the country set aside for them in the West by previous treaties. The United States agreed to pay $5 million, cover the cost of various claims levied by and against the Cherokees, appraise and compensate for the value of all improvements left behind, set aside money for schools, orphans, and a national fund, and pay the cost of removal to and subsistence in the West during the first year. The Cherokees had two years from the date of ratification to prepare for the migration, during which time the United States promised to protect them in the use of their farms, homes, and businesses. The United States also agreed to add an eight-hundred-thousand-acre tract to the seven million acres of western territory already assigned and provide a patent to the Nation in fee simple ownership for the whole. The Cherokee Nation received assurances that the United States would respect its right to self-government in the West, that the Nation could never be included into any state or territory without its consent, and that the United States would protect its borders, remove unwanted American intruders, and defend the Cherokees from hostile neighbors. And in order to "secure . . . the rights guarantied to them in this treaty, . . . they shall be entitled to a delegate in the House of Representatives of the United States whenever Congress shall make provision for the same."[16] After some last-minute adjustments, the president submitted the treaty to the Senate for ratification. Having already defeated one treaty concluded with an unauthorized group of Cherokees, Ross had reason to hope that this one could be scuttled as well. Despite his best efforts and the petition containing the names of thousands of angry Cherokees, he failed. With one vote more than the necessary two-thirds majority, the Senate approved the Treaty of New Echota in May 1836. President Jackson proclaimed it ratified on May 23, thereby setting the date for removal at May 23, 1838.

Following the proclamation of the treaty, Ross worked to overturn it. In the summer of 1836, he wrote a pamphlet for circulation in the East that criticized the treaty and the illegal gathering of men who had negotiated it. In the fall the General Council declared the treaty null and void and appointed Ross to head a delegation to the western Cherokees, who had already removed, to enlist their help in fighting it. At the head of a delegation representing the two groups of Cherokees, Ross reached Washington in February 1837, shortly before the Jackson government left office. The outgoing officials would have nothing to do with him, but once Martin Van Buren took office, his secretary of war, Joel Poinsett, contacted Ross to enlist his aid in negotiating an end to the Second Seminole War. Expecting a favorable reward from the new government, Ross acquiesced with a letter to the Seminoles urging them to stop fighting. Carried by four Cherokee emissaries, the effort was a fiasco. Poinsett, however, did listen to Ross's ideas about the treaty. Van Buren refused to consider negotiating a new one, despite Ross's unceasing efforts to do so, but Poinsett agreed to increase some of the payments. In early 1838, just weeks before removal was scheduled to commence, he accepted Ross's request to permit the Cherokees to manage removal themselves.

No one could look at the history of the Treaty of New Echota and conclude that it was honestly and fairly made by the United States with the Cherokee Nation. Even Georgia governor William Schley, successor to Wilson Lumpkin and a close political ally, admitted that it was "not made with the sanction of their leaders."[17] Both John and Major Ridge were later quoted as announcing as they signed the document that they were signing their death warrants for having violated the Cherokee law against the sale of the land by unauthorized persons. But Georgia wanted the Cherokees out of the state, Jackson wanted them out of the country east of the Mississippi, and Ridge and his supporters in the "treaty party" believed that they knew better than the Cherokee government how best to end the suffering of the Cherokee people. In one unholy fit of collusion, neither law nor morality could be allowed to hinder the removal of the Cherokees. This was neither the first nor the last time that good men did bad things in the name of their love for the people.

6

THE TRAIL OF TEARS

❈

IN LATE SUMMER 1838 a detachment of Cherokees began to exit the stockade where they had been held for
months awaiting the long journey to their new home west of
the Mississippi. "At this very moment a low sound of distant
thunder fell on my ear," recalled Cherokee William Shorey
Coodey. "In almost an exact western direction a dark spiral
cloud was rising above the horizon and sent forth a murmur
I almost fancied a voice of divine indignation for the wrongs
of my poor and unhappy countrymen, driven by *brutal*
power from all they loved and cherished in the land of their
fathers, to gratify the cravings of avarice." Coodey and others
who witnessed the incident regarded it as an omen.[1] By the
time the Cherokees had reached their new home in the West,
any doubt that the dark cloud portended tragedy had been
dispelled.

In the history of interaction between Euro-Americans and Indians, Cherokee removal was not an isolated event. The involuntary relocation of Native people had long been an aspect of United States policy. Throughout the East, when Indian people surrendered their land as a result of sale or defeat in war, they moved farther west. In the process, they encroached on the territory of other Indian nations, who often resisted. Early Cherokee migrants to Arkansas, for example, confronted opposition from the Osage in whose traditional homeland they settled, and they ultimately forced the Osage to surrender part of their territory. Furthermore, Cherokee removal was only part of a much broader plan to rid the eastern United States of Indians. By the end of the nineteenth century, over sixty tribes, mostly from the East, had been exiled to Oklahoma. Native people in the Midwest as well as the Cherokees' neighbors in the South shared the experience of expulsion. Before the Cherokees began their forced migration to the West, most Choctaws, Creeks, and Chickasaws as well as many Seminoles already had endured their own trails of tears. Although their experiences are not generally as well known, their suffering equaled that of the Cherokees.[2]

Cherokee removal did not take place as a single deportation of people but instead spanned many years. Small groups of Cherokees had begun relocating to the West voluntarily as early as 1794. In 1810–11, following a land cession in the East, approximately one thousand Cherokees moved to what is today Arkansas, and in 1819 another land cession sent two thousand Cherokees to merge with them. These removals, however, were voluntary, and the Cherokees who went west before the Treaty of New Echota often returned to their homeland in the East to visit family and friends and to reconnect to the land that formed the touchstone of their identity as Cherokees.

In 1828 the western Cherokees ceded their land in Arkansas and moved into what is today northeastern Oklahoma. A provision in the 1828 treaty provided for their eastern brethren to join them. Every head of family living in Georgia or other states that wanted to expel them was to receive "a good Rifle, a Blanket, a Kettle, and five pounds of Tobacco" when he or she enrolled for removal. The treaty promised a blanket to each family member as well. The United States pledged to provide compensation for property left behind, transportation to the West, and twelve months of support upon their arrival. Furthermore, every person who brought along four other Cherokees from the state of Georgia would receive fifty dollars.[3] The Cherokees' agent employed two western Cherokees to encourage emigration, but they met with considerable opposition and hostility. After six months, the agent had managed to enroll only eleven families. Following the passage of the Georgia law in 1828 that extended state jurisdiction over the Cherokee Nation (beginning in 1830), enrollment picked up a bit, but most of these enrollees were intermarried whites, their families, and their slaves. They usually traveled on steamboats provided by the United States, but they suffered from a scarcity of supplies and price gouging by speculators. Some eventually returned to the East, and stories of their ordeal stiffened the Cherokees' resolve to remain in their homeland.

When Congress passed the Indian Removal Act in 1830, President Jackson suspended enrollment in the hope of increasing pressure on the Cherokees for a land cession and wholesale removal. In the summer of 1831, Governor Gilmer of Georgia asked Jackson to reinstate enrollment because he thought that perhaps the misery of the Cherokees had reached the point that they would gladly go west. Jackson complied, but the agent he appointed had little success in persuading Cherokees. By the end of the year, he had enrolled only seventy-one families, and nearly a third were those of intermarried whites. Severe winter privation prompted some additional Cherokees to enroll, but the agent's total for his first year was 683 Cherokees, 47 intermarried whites, and 193 African-American slaves out of a population of approximately 17,000.[4] The Supreme Court's favorable decision in *Worcester* v. *Georgia* and the hope that Henry Clay would defeat Jackson in the election of 1832 dimmed the prospect of enrolling many more.

Jackson won the election and ignored the Court, however, and Georgia tightened the screws on the Cherokees. As winners in the Georgia land lottery began to put some Cherokees out of their homes, the situation grew more desperate, but several factors put a damper on enrollment. First of all, the western Cherokees complained that the United States had not fulfilled the terms of the 1828 treaty that moved them from Arkansas to Indian Territory and that their resources were too limited to absorb the emigrants. They asked for an increase in their annuities and an enlargement of their territory, but the request was ignored. Second, a cholera epidemic discouraged all travel in the West. And finally, Cherokee officials actively opposed people emigrating. By 1833 the agreement that enrollees signed not only included the provision for goods from the Treaty of 1828 but also promised them before departure their share of the three years of annuity payments that the United States had withheld and of other annuities from past and future treaties. Improved terms did not produce much better results: Eight hundred people who enrolled to go west reneged on the agreement.

The approximately nine hundred who embarked in the spring of 1834 endured many trials. Even before they left the dock on flatboats the United States had provided, unscrupulous traders arrived on their own boats and moored on the riverbank opposite the agency. From there, they hawked "cakes and pies and fruit and cider and apple jack and whiskey" in order to relieve the Cherokees of the annuity payments they had received. The lieutenant appointed conductor of one of the detachments protested that the boats were the "nurseries and receptacles of idleness, drunkenness, and vice." Then measles, which few of the emigrants had had, broke out. When the departure date finally arrived, "many a manly cheek [was] suffused with tears." The party had no major disasters until they began ascending the Arkansas River. Shoals and low water forced them to abandon some of their provisions, but that was not sufficient, so soon they had to unload the boats and prepare to continue on land. Then cholera struck. The lieutenant recorded in his journal, "At one time I saw stretched around me and in a few feet of each other, eight of these afflicted creatures dead or dying." Ultimately eighty-one people in the party died, fifty of them from cholera. Some survivors lost virtually their entire families. Black Fox (not the former principal chief), for example, lost his wife and three children. "There is a dignity in their grief which is sublime," the lieutenant conceded, "and which, poor and destitute, ignorant and unbefriended as they were, made me respect them."[5]

The negotiations that led to the Treaty of New Echota and the outrage that followed largely halted emigration. The United States, fearing an Indian uprising, sent Brigadier General John E. Wool and two thousand soldiers to the Cherokee Nation to disarm the Cherokees and encourage them to enroll. He pleaded with the Cherokees to go west: "Why not abandon a country no longer yours? Do you not see the white people daily coming into it, driving you from your homes and possessing your houses, your cornfields and your ferries?"[6] He warned that soon he would be unable to offer them protection against these intruders. Nevertheless, most Cherokees persisted in their opposition to enrollment.

The next party to embark was composed of approximately six hundred members of the Treaty Party. They received authorization and payment to conduct their own removal, and early in 1837 they departed the East in relative comfort with their livestock and slaves. Major Ridge and his family had intended to join this party, but poor health forced him to postpone. Instead he joined a detachment of 466 people who started their journey on March 3. Although Major Ridge and his family began the trip on open boats, as soon as the detachment boarded a steamboat, they moved into a cabin. In Decatur, Alabama, low water forced the detachment to land. The Tuscumbia, Courtland, and Decatur Railroad, the first rail line west of the Appalachians, transported them to Tuscumbia where they boarded keelboats for the rest of their journey. A missionary who had watched their departure from their homeland wrote: "It is mournful to see how these people go away—even the stoutest hearts melt into tears when they turn their faces towards the setting sun—and I am sure that this land will be bedewed with a Nation's tears—if not with their blood."[7] Major Ridge's detachment spilled only tears, arriving in the West before the end of the month without casualties.

The next detachment was not as fortunate. Leaving the Cherokee Agency on October 14, 1837, the 365 emigrants suffered terribly from rain, snow, and sickness. On December 17, the officer in charge of the detachment wrote in his journal: "Snowed last night. Buried Elleges wife, and Charles Timberlakes son, Smoker. Marched at 9 o'c A.M. halted at Mr. Dyes. 3 o'c, extremely cold, sickness prevailing to a considerable extent. All very much fatigued, encamped issued corn and fodder, and beef. 10 miles today."[8] Other days were distressingly similar. Finally, on December 30, the detachment arrived in the Cherokees' new country and disbanded.

The fifteen who had died en route included eleven children, eight of them under two years of age.

According to the terms of the Treaty of New Echota, the Cherokees had to relinquish their territory in the East within two years of ratification. After that deadline, they faced eviction by force. Deeply attached to their homeland and terrified by the difficulties earlier emigrants had encountered, many Cherokees made no preparations to leave. Furthermore, Chief Ross and a delegation were in Washington trying to negotiate a new treaty that would give them additional time and permit the Nation to remove itself. By May 1838, time was up, and only two thousand Cherokees had removed. General Winfield Scott assumed command of the seven thousand soldiers, militia, and volunteers who had assembled to evict the Cherokees and set up headquarters at New Echota. On May 10, he issued a proclamation ordering the Cherokee people to start vacating their homeland within the month. Recognizing that a sudden change of heart on the part of the Cherokees was unlikely, Scott began to build thirty-one forts near Cherokee towns.

When the deadline of May 23 passed and the Cherokees had not begun to move, the soldiers began rounding them up and confining them in the forts. Troops quickly captured most Cherokees. When a widow named Ooloocha filed a claim for her abandoned property in Georgia in 1842, she recounted the experience: "The soldiers came and took us from home. They first surrounded our house and they took the mare while we were at work in the fields and they drove us out of doors and did not permit us to take anything with us not even a second change of clothes, only the clothes we had on, and they shut the doors after they turned us out. They would not permit any of us to enter the house to get any clothing but drove us off to a fort that was built at New Echota. They kept us in the fort about three days and then marched us to Ross's Landing. And still on foot, even our little children, and they kept us about three days at Ross's Landing and sent us off on a boat to this country [Indian Territory]."[9] In the 1930s Rebecca Neugin, who was a small child during removal, recalled the terror of the roundup: "When the soldiers came to our house my father wanted to fight, but my mother told him that the soldiers would kill him if he did and we surrendered without a fight. They drove us out of our house to join the other prisoners in a stockade." Like Ooloocha and other Cherokees, Neugin's family had not been able to take any provisions with them: "After they took us away my mother begged them to let her go back and get some bedding. So they let her go back and she brought what bedding and a few cooking utensils she could carry and had to leave behind all of our other household possessions."[10] The Cherokees left their corn growing in the fields and, on occasion, dinner on the table. Stories abound of families separated in the roundup. Parents away from home or children at play might return to find an empty house. Missionary Daniel Butrick reported that two small children ran to the woods when the soldiers approached. Their mother begged permission to search for them, but the soldiers refused. Only much later did they permit a family friend to return and search for them. Tik-i-kiski, who was over a hundred years old, was left behind because the soldiers had no conveyance for him, but they took his entire family. He nearly starved to death, but some white children found him and brought him food. Finally he was reunited with his family at the stockade. A deaf man failed to respond to the soldiers' commands, and they shot him dead. Greedy whites often witnessed these scenes because they had flocked to the Cherokee Nation "to seize whatever property they could put their hands on."[11]

Conditions in the forts were abysmal. Missionary Daniel Butrick protested that the Cherokees were first kept in such close quarters and under such intense guard that it was "impossible for male or female to secrete themselves from the gaze of the multitudes for any purpose whatever, unless by hanging up some cloth in their tents, and there they had no vessel for private use." Whiskey dealers and card sharks lurked nearby, and in their desperation, some Cherokees succumbed to temptation. Alcohol-induced violence became a growing problem in the forts. Other Cherokees exhibited considerable fortitude and attempted to conduct themselves with decorum. Two Baptist converts held church services at Fort Butler in North Carolina and received permission from the commander to baptize ten converts in the nearby river. As soon as possible, Scott moved the Cherokees from the forts to eleven internment camps near the western boundary of the Cherokee Nation in preparation for their deportation. While in transit, Butrick wrote in his journal, they "were obliged at night to lie down on the naked ground, in the open air, exposed to wind and rain, and herd[ed] together, men women and children, like droves of hogs, and in this way, many are hastening to a premature grave."[12]

General Scott exempted one group of Cherokees from the roundup—the Oconaluftee Cherokees in western North Carolina. The treaty of 1819 ceded the land on which they lived and, rather than relocate within the new boundaries of the Cherokee Nation, they had taken 640-acre reservations and become citizens of the state of North Carolina. In 1837 the North Carolina legislature and the federal government acknowledged the right of the Oconaluftee Cherokees to remain. These Cherokees lived near the Cherokee Nation, and they had friends and relatives who did not qualify for their exemption. Some of these took refuge in the mountains when Scott began his roundup. The fugitives suffered from want of food and shelter, and by fall many of them were starving. Materially unable to offer much help, the Oconaluftees also feared that these fugitives might jeopardize their right to remain in North Carolina.[13]

Conditions in the camps marked little improvement over those in the forts except that the camps were larger. The army issued rations, but the food and living conditions were so different from what the Cherokees were accustomed to that many sickened and died. Physicians were available, but the language barrier and the Cherokee preference for their own healers meant that few people availed themselves of their services. Dysentery and fever were rampant, and there were outbreaks of whooping cough and measles. Furthermore, unscrupulous whites preyed on the dispirited people. Butrick remonstrated that "the poor Cherokees are not only exposed to temporal evils, but also to every species of moral desolation." In the camps, alcohol was still readily available to both Cherokees and soldiers. Butrick expressed particular concern about the sexual abuse of women. Soldiers caught one young married woman, dragged her about the camp, forced her to drink with them, and "then seduced her away. . . . How many of the poor captive women are thus debauched, through terror and seduction, that eye which never sleeps alone can determine."[14]

In early June Scott divided 2,800 Cherokees into three detachments and prepared for their immediate departure by water, a prospect made even more terrifying by the drowning of over 300 Creeks the previous year during their transportation to the West. On June 6 the first party of approximately 800 Cherokees embarked by boat from Ross's Landing (Chattanooga) followed by 875 more on June 13. Butrick wrote in his journal that the people in the first detachment were "literally crammed into the boat [which] . . . was so filled that the timbers began to crack and give way, and the boat itself was on the point of sinking." Ultimately, six flatboats were lashed to a steamboat for the trip down the Tennessee River to Decatur, Alabama. Butrick saw the second detachment "driven to the bank of the river, and there guarded all night, to lie down like so many animals on the naked ground."[15] They, too, departed on six flatboats, but they picked up two additional boats and more Cherokees downriver. At Decatur,

Indians from both detachments were loaded onto railroad cars, which took them to Tuscumbia. Then they resumed their water route, traveling down the Tennessee, Ohio, and Mississippi rivers and then up the Arkansas as far as they could. Drought made river navigation increasingly difficult as the summer wore on, and the second detachment actually entered Indian Territory by wagon. The first detachment suffered no deaths en route; the second counted seventy. As the summer heat and drought intensified, their suffering increased, and, according to missionary Cephas Washburn, "much sickness and mortality" persisted after their arrival in their new home.[16]

On June 11, a group of confined Cherokees petitioned to be permitted to remain in the East "till the sickly time is over." They warned, "If you send the whole nation, the whole nation will die."[17] But orders went out for the third detachment to depart. As they made their way along the riverbank, a woman in labor collapsed. A soldier stabbed her with a bayonet, and she soon died.[18] The detachment had just gotten under way on June 17 when word arrived that Secretary of War Joel Poinsett had agreed in principle to the Cherokees' removing themselves. He also had determined that the best time for them to leave for the West was September, a decision that required them to delay their departure from the East for months. The nature of communication—it took about two weeks for letters to go back and forth to Washington—meant that Poinsett did not realize that thousands of Cherokees already had been captured, imprisoned, and deported.

When the third detachment got word of the brief reprieve, its members demanded to be permitted to return to their homes. The officer in charge refused, and the Cherokees began to run away. The army called on local citizens to help apprehend the fugitives, but approximately three hundred remained at large. The others struggled on to Indian Territory. Instead of embarking on boats at Ross's Landing, the detachment traveled overland two hundred miles across northern Alabama before boarding boats at Waterloo on the state's northwestern border. The officer in charge wrote, "Verry many of this party were about naked, barefoot and suffering with fatigue." They could travel only about nine miles a day, so he put the old and infirm on boats to Decatur while the others continued on foot.[19] Despite their suffering, this detachment committed acts of civil disobedience: They refused to give their names to the muster officer or to accept clothing proffered by the emigration agent.

Heat and drought limited the food and water supply en route, so General Scott consented to a postponement of further removals until September. But he insisted that the Cherokees, with a few exceptions, remain in the camps. The protracted heat wave prevented further detachments from starting for the West until October, a situation that left the Cherokees living in deplorable conditions in the camps. One of the casualties was the ninety-year-old former slave of a Cherokee planter named Sanders. Her children Nanny and Peter had managed to save enough money working after hours to purchase her freedom just before she died. They, however, remained in bondage, and

Sanders sold Peter and his wife to slave traders before the Cherokees left the East. Perhaps they would have preferred removal.[20]

Poinsett ordered Scott to let the Cherokees conduct their own removal. John Ross became the superintendent for removal, and the delegation that had just returned from Washington formed a removal committee. The committee estimated the expense of removing the Cherokees at $65,880 per thousand. General Scott termed the figure "extravagant." The committee had recommended one wagon and five saddle horses for every twenty people. Scott insisted that those who were so sick that they needed conveyance and "heavy articles of property" be left behind until they could be transported by riverboats. Furthermore, he pointed out, among one thousand people, "there are at least 500 strong men, women, girls and boys not only capable of marching twelve or fifteen miles a day, but to whom the exercise would be beneficial." He conceded, however, that the funds that Congress appropriated for removal belonged to the Cherokee Nation, and grudgingly approved the estimate.[21]

When the removal committee designated Lewis Ross, brother of the principal chief, to be the contacting agent for removal, Scott exploded. Ross was a prominent merchant who had the expertise and contacts to provision the Cherokees, but local whites complained bitterly about the arrangement because it deprived them of the lucrative business of contracting to supply the horses, wagons, blankets, and food for removal. "The contract with Mr. Lewis Ross, was entered into without any knowledge on my part," Scott fumed. He predicted an "enormous profit" for Ross, which never materialized. Furthermore, "highly respectable citizens" had not been permitted to bid on the contract.[22] The committee members responded that "they had no wish to invite the competition of white contractors, not responsible to themselves, nor answerable to their laws." The Cherokees were interested in far more than the bottom line: "The lives and health and comfort of our people, are, with us points of paramount consideration." Finally, they reminded him that the Cherokees were now in charge of their own removal.[23] There was nothing Scott could do.

The prolonged drought restricted the navigability of the rivers taken by earlier detachments, so the Cherokees had no alternative but to go by land. Ross organized them into thirteen detachments of approximately one thousand people each, and the council appointed a conductor and assistant for each detachment. A physician, interpreter, wagon master, and commissary agent also was assigned to each. Ten or twelve Cherokees served as a Light Horse Guard for each detachment. Their primary responsibility was to keep internal order and assist in managing the detachment; they had no authority to protect the Cherokees from whites.

Having delayed a month at Blythe's Ferry, the first detachment left the Cherokee Nation at the end of September 1838, others followed in October, and the last four departed in November. The soldiers had refused to permit most people to bring their belongings. Rebecca Neugin recalled that other families had to borrow the cooking utensils that her mother had retrieved. Since people had been forced into the camps in summer, many did not have appropriate clothes. As the first detachment departed, leaders wrote Chief Ross that two-thirds were in "destitute condition." They needed shoes, blankets, and clothing, and they had only eighty-three tents for over a thousand people.[24] They stopped in Nashville, as did other detachments, and Lewis Ross provided them with the supplies they needed for the rest of the way. Because the journey lasted longer than anticipated and the conditions were more severe, Ross had to purchase additional provisions along the way.

Most detachments took roughly the same route—to Nashville, Tennessee, and then to Hopkinsville, Kentucky. They traversed southern Illinois and took a ferry across the Mississippi in the vicinity of Cape Girardeau. Having crossed Missouri through Rolla and Springfield, they turned south to Fayetteville, Arkansas, and then west before they finally arrived in their new home. Detachments on this route traveled 826 miles. There were, however, several deviations: John Benge's detachment traveled a more southerly route of 734 miles that passed through Batesville, Arkansas, and Peter Hildebrand's detachment went south of Rolla but reconnected with the main route before it reached Springfield.[25] The final land parties went somewhat farther north, because earlier detachments had depleted the countryside of game, which men killed to supplement the rations. The journey took three to six months. A final party of about 230 Cherokees who were too old and sick to make the journey by land left by boat in early December after water levels had risen. John Ross, who had stayed to supervise the earlier departures, and his family were in this group.

There were no widespread desertions from the detachments as there had been in those that departed during the summer under army escort—Ross reported a total of 182 for the thirteen detachments—but one group of North Carolina Cherokees did abscond and join the fugitives in the mountains. General Scott dispatched troops to bring them in, and soldiers captured a Cherokee named Tsali, his family, and several others. On the way to headquarters, the Cherokees killed two of the four soldiers, wounded a third, and fled into the mountains. William Holland Thomas, an adopted white man who served as agent for the Oconaluftee Cherokees, enlisted the aid of Euchella, a Cherokee who had been in hiding, to find Tsali's party. Euchella and his men succeeded: By the end of November, they had captured everyone in the group and had executed Tsali, his brother, and two of his sons for the deaths of the soldiers. Satisfied with the outcome, the army left the mountains and the other fugitives, the treaty commissioners permitted Euchella's band to stay with the Oconaluftees, and the executions secured the Oconaluftees' treaty right to remain in their homeland, where their descendants are recognized today as the Eastern Band of Cherokee Indians.[26]

Those Cherokees forced from their homeland departed with heavy hearts. Cherokee George Hicks lamented, "We are now about to take our final leave and kind farewell to our native land the country that the Great Spirit gave our Fathers, we are on the eve of leaving that Country that gave us birth."[27] For Cherokees, the land had meaning far deeper than its commercial value. Their creation as a people tied them to this place, and now they were being compelled to surrender it and march west, the direction associated with death. A traveler from Maine who encountered detachments of Cherokees in western Kentucky described the ways Cherokees coped with their situation: "The Indians as a whole carry in their countenances every thing but the appearance of happiness. Some carry a downcast dejected look bordering upon the appearance of despair; others a wild frantic appearance as if about to burst the chains of nature and pounce like a tiger upon their enemies." Above all, they had lost faith in the United States. In one Kentucky town, a local resident asked an elderly Indian man if he remembered him from his service with the United States Army in the Creek War. The old man replied, "Ah! My life and the lives of my people were then at stake for you and your country. I then thought Jackson my best friend. But ah! Jackson no serve me right. Your country no do me justice now!"[28]

The permanent relocation of thirteen thousand people over a distance of nearly a thousand miles would be a daunting task even in the twenty-first century, and conditions in the nineteenth century made it excruciating. The roads were dirt, and when the rains finally came in November, they became nearly impassable. In hilly terrain, which describes much of their route, the Cherokees often had to double-team horses to pull the wagons up steep inclines. Many roads required the payment of tolls, and while some gatekeepers showed compassion, others fleeced the emigrants. Several detachments veered slightly off the established route to avoid toll gates. The detachments crossed rivers on ferries whose operation depended on river conditions. Early detachments had to wait for the Tennessee River to rise at Blythe's Ferry before they could get under way, and ice floes in the Mississippi halted several detachments for as long as a month. Even under optimum conditions, crossing rivers was a slow process. When Peter Hildebrand's detachment departed on November 12, it took two and a half days for the 1,766 people, eighty-eight wagons, 881 horses, and a number of oxen to cross the Tennessee River. Four boats worked from dawn to dusk transporting the detachment.

Agents secured campsites in advance. Located at intervals of ten to fifteen miles, a day's journey, the sites ideally had sufficient water for drinking, wood for fires, and grass for livestock. Sometimes detachments could not get as far as they had intended, and property owners refused them permission to camp or collect firewood. Danger often stalked Cherokees who did not camp at authorized sites or wandered away from detachments. Missionary Butrick reported that an elderly man who fell behind in Illinois was found dead by local whites, who buried him and then filed suit against the leader of the closest detachment for the cost of the burial. Butrick speculated that the man who filed suit was also the one responsible for the old man's death. Two young men who "had a considerable amount of property" were found dead after they stopped off in Golconda as their detachment went on.[29]

Horses and oxen were essential to the detachments, but they consumed an enormous quantity of grain and forage. The removal committee had estimated sixteen cents per day for human rations and forty cents for horses, which ate an average of 140 bushels of corn per day per detachment. The plan originally was to transport this food between provisioning stations, but most detachments did not have enough wagons to carry forage and the people who needed transport. Jesse Bushyhead wrote Ross that the only solution for his detachment was "hauling forage to the place designated, and then returning for the people."[30] As the journey progressed, the situation became more critical, and conductors had to resort to purchasing corn locally at exorbitant prices. Grazing helped relieve the problem, although the drought limited pasturage, and Bushyhead's detachment was delayed further when his oxen sickened from eating poison ivy. Food was not the only problem involving livestock. Whites stopped the Cherokees on the march and demanded horses in payment of unsubstantiated debts. The Light Horse Guard could do nothing to protect the Cherokees' property from such thieves.

Most Cherokees, however, did not ride in wagons or on horseback—they walked. Rebecca Neugin's father had a wagon and two teams of oxen, but her parents and older brother walked the entire way. The traveler from Maine passed several detachments, one of which stretched for three miles, and reported: "A great many go on horseback and multitudes on foot—even aged females, apparently nearly ready to drop into the grave, were traveling with heavy burdens attached to the back—on the sometimes frozen ground, and sometimes muddy streets, with no covering for the feet except what nature had given them."[31]

Shelter and subsistence presented a number of problems. Cherokees often had to pitch their canvas tents in howling wind, torrential rain, brutal cold, and heavy snow. Food was monotonous—largely dried corn, which had to be ground, and salt pork. Occasionally Ross's agents were able to locate supplies of beef, and men hunted game along the road. Rebecca Neugin recalled: "The people were so tired of eating salt pork on the journey that my father would walk through the woods as we traveled, hunting for turkeys and deer which he brought into camp to feed us." Drinking water was a constant worry: Drought had made water scarce and its quality questionable. Some detachments delayed their journey in central Tennessee because streams had dried up and there were no wells. The venerable chief White Path died after drinking from what was presumably a tainted well as his detachment crossed Kentucky.

Exposure and fatigue weakened immune systems, making people susceptible to disease and making their recovery doubtful. Measles and whooping cough as well as dysentery and respiratory infections swept through the detachments. Although physicians accompanied the detachments, they were often overwhelmed by marching all day and treating the sick at night. Cherokee doctors faced additional problems, as oral tradition recorded in the 1930s suggests: "The Indian Doctors couldn't find the herbs they were use to and didn't know the ones they did find, so they couldn't doctor them as they would have at home."[32] When people could no longer walk, conductors had to make room for them in the wagons. The Maine traveler observed that the wagons carrying "the sick and feeble were . . . about as comfortable for traveling as a New England ox cart with a covering over it." Children and elders died in disproportionate numbers. A wealthy Cherokee couple passed the traveler in their fashionable carriage, but even they were not exempt from hardship and grief: They buried their youngest child a few miles down the road and then continued, leaving the small grave behind.[33] Rebecca Neugin remembered that "there was much sickness and a great many little children died of whooping cough."[34] No one was immune. Just after disembarking at Little Rock to continue overland, Chief Ross buried his wife.

The journals from the removal of 1838–39 are distressingly similar to the ones from earlier emigrations, suggesting that proponents of removal should have known what the consequences would be. Missionary Butrick, who along with his wife accompanied the Cherokees on the Trail of Tears, recorded in his journal on December 13, 1838, "Sixty persons had died out of their [Bushyhead's] detachment previous to their arrival at that place. During the night a Cherokee woman died in the camps. Though she had given birth to a child but a few days before, yet last evening she was up, & no danger was apprehended, but in the morning she was found dead with the infant in her arms. As the man living near was not willing to have her buried there, . . . the corpse was carried all day in the wagon. . . . Also on Saturday night of last week an infant, a few months old, died with the bowel complaint. . . . Near the place of the [church] meeting was a man sitting by a fire, afflicted with the bowel complaint. . . . Yesterday about noon he died. . . . He was a professor of religion. . . . The young man burnt on the mountain, when drunk is dead."[35] Death did not distinguish between young and old, good and bad.

The number of Cherokees who perished on the Trail of Tears probably will never be known. The most commonly cited figure for deaths is 4,000, or approximately one-quarter of the Cherokees, an estimate made by Dr. Elizur Butler, a missionary who accompanied the Cherokees. By his own count, John Ross supervised the removal of 13,149, and his detachments reported 424 deaths and 69 births along with 182 desertions. A United States official in Indian Territory counted 11,504 arrivals, a discrepancy of 1,645 when compared to Ross's total of those who departed the East. Neither figure takes into account voluntary emigrations or Cherokees removed by the army in the summer of 1838. Furthermore, many uncounted Cherokees died in the camps during the summer of 1838 while awaiting removal. Sociologist Russell Thornton has speculated that removal cost the Cherokees 10,000 individuals between 1835 and 1840, including the children that victims would have produced had they survived.

Therefore, the overall demographic effect was far greater than the actual number of casualties.[36] Measuring the disaster in terms of the number of casualties, however, is a mistake. If only one Cherokee had died—or none at all—the dispossession and deportation of thousands of people from their homeland under a fraudulent treaty would still be a tragedy. The dark cloud that appeared as they left the East may well be regarded as an omen of that tragedy.

7

REBUILDING IN THE WEST

⊛

"THE COUNTRY is in such a state just now that there seems little encouragement for people to build good houses or make anything," Jane Ross Meigs wrote her father, Chief John Ross, who was in Washington, in November 1845. "I am so nervous I can scarce write at all. I hope it will not be long you'll be at home but I hope the country will be settled by that time too."[1] The fear and anguish so evident in Meigs's letter cut across the political chasm that divided the Cherokee Nation. Less than a year later Sarah Watie of the Treaty Party wrote her husband, Stand, "I am so tired of living this way. I don't believe I could live one year longer if I knew that we could not get settled, it has wore my spirits out just the thoughts of not having a good home. . . . I am perfectly sick of the world."[2] A decade after the signing and ratification of the Treaty of New Echota, the Cherokee Nation was still in

Jane Ross Meigs Nave, the daughter of Chief John Ross, lost her home when political enemies set fire to it in 1845 in an attempt to kill her first husband, R. J. Meigs. From Edmund Schwarze, History of the Moravian Missions among Southern Indian Tribes of the United States *(Bethlehem, Pa.: Times Publishing Company, 1923); copy in the North Carolina Collection, Wilson Library, University of North Carolina, Chapel Hill.*

turmoil. Having taken the Cherokees' land and forced them to march across a third of the continent, the United States now further threatened the Cherokees' sovereignty and existence as a people.

The Cherokees arrived in Indian Territory exhausted and dispirited. Under the terms of the Treaty of New Echota, the United States was supposed to provide rations for a year. The United States advertised for bids in Arkansas and Missouri newspapers, but controversy surrounded the awarding of contracts, not only for Cherokee provisions but also for those provided other displaced Indians. Potential contractors usually banded together to bid up the price and then joined in providing the rations at exorbitant rates. Sometimes, corrupt U.S. officials entirely dispensed with the bidding process.

Rations included meat, grain for bread, and salt. The daily allowance was three-fourths pound of salt pork or fresh beef, one pound of wheat flour or three-fourths quart of corn, and four quarts of salt per one hundred rations. Normally, contractors distributed rations every other month, which constituted a real problem for people living in tents without proper storage facilities. The day appointed for distribution varied from time to time so that some families arrived to receive rations only to have to wait another two weeks for provisions to be delivered. United States agents often were absent during the allocation of goods, one because he was a "confirmed drunkard" and two others because of "dissipated habits."[3] Not surprisingly, fraud was widespread. The poorest Cherokees, those who desperately needed the goods, often camped at the distribution site and received their rations at daylight before wealthier Cherokees, who had breakfast in their homes, arrived on the scene. According to one observer, "That course was adopted to prevent the interference of the better or more intelligent class of Cherokees, who had made considerable efforts to protect the others from imposition."[4]

The rations were not sufficient, partly because most Cherokees had little means to keep or supplement them, but primarily because dishonest contractors did not supply what they had promised. Corn arrived on the cob, often after a lengthy overland journey during which many of the dried kernels rubbed off the cobs. Contractors doled out the corn to the Cherokees as though the cobs were full, thereby depriving them of a substantial portion of their grain allowance. According to one estimate, the contractors cheated Cherokees of one bushel out of every ten of corn. The Cherokees complained about the quality of the beef and insisted, as the weather turned warm, that it was unhealthy to eat fresh meat. Instead, they demanded salt pork. Furthermore, the cattle had had little pasturage in the fall and winter of 1838–39, so they were quite emaciated by the spring, providing mostly bones and little meat to hungry Cherokees. Contractors took advantage of the opportunity to dispose of cattle that no one else would buy, so the Cherokees got a disproportionate number of old bulls and even one ancient blind ox. Some Cherokees who tried to keep the cattle on the hoof long enough to fatten them up discovered that contractors would steal the animals and reissue them. In the absence of scales, contractors consistently overestimated the weight of cattle. They received $3.87½ per month for each ration; half of this amount (or slightly over $1.93) was for meat, but contractors normally paid one dollar per month for a ration of meat, which would have resulted in enormous profits even if quality and quantity had been as promised.

Cherokees usually had little say over the meat they received. Contractors took up the tickets that entitled them to rations, then issued the meat, and, if the recipients did not like what was issued, simply told them to take it or leave it. Some Cherokees sold their ration tickets for as little as one cent a pound and then used that meager amount to buy better-quality food. But food prices in Indian Territory were very high, so many could not afford market prices. Liquor, however, was a bargain. Although Cherokee and federal law prohibited its sale to Indians, many Cherokees tried to drown their sorrows in all too readily available alcohol.

The early years in Indian Territory were extraordinarily hard.[5] Most Cherokees arrived with little livestock or farming equipment. Those who came west in the Ross detachments also discovered that the Cherokees who had arrived earlier had laid claim to the best land. While northeastern Oklahoma looks superficially like the Cherokees' homeland in the Southeast—there are steep, forested hills and fast-flowing streams—farming conditions were quite different. Cherokees who cleared land along rivers soon discovered that the shallow braided streams frequently flooded, washing away their crops. Furthermore, the soil was much more difficult to till and required a heavy plow pulled by two horses. Cherokee families were lucky to have one horse, so they planted their crops more shallowly, but this practice made them more susceptible to the intense heat of Indian Territory summers. Continuing drought parched their plants, and plagues of grasshoppers devoured what was left.

Political divisions made coping with economic problems far more difficult. When the Ross detachments arrived in the spring of 1839, they joined two other distinct groups—the Old Settlers who had emigrated before the Treaty of New Echota and the Treaty Party that left before the forcible removal of 1838–39. There were roughly 3,000 Old Settlers, 2,000 Treaty Party members, and 14,000 in Ross's detachments. Melding these groups into one polity was a daunting task.

In August 1838 as they were preparing to leave their homeland, the Cherokees met in Council at Aquohee and enacted a resolution that would have important implications for their Nation. First of all, they affirmed that "the title of the Cherokee people to their land is the most ancient, pure, and absolute known to man," and they insisted that "the original title and ownership of said lands still rest in the Cherokee Nation." They denied that either they or their representatives had legitimately parted with the land. Second, they maintained that the United States was responsible for reimbursing individuals for property they had lost and that individual acceptance of payment in no way compromised the Nation's claim to the land. Third, they declared that "the inherent sovereignty of the Cherokee Nation, together with the constitution, laws, and useages, of the same, . . . shall continue so to be in perpetuity."[6] That is, they agreed to transfer their government to the West. The problem was that the Old Settlers had their own government and laws.

In June 1839, between six and seven thousand Cherokees assembled at Takatoka Camp Ground to resolve the looming political crisis. John Brown, the principal chief of the Old Settlers, welcomed the emigrants and invited them to participate in the upcoming election, but until then, he insisted, the new arrivals would be subject to the Old Settlers' government and laws. In his address to the council, John Ross characterized those present as "of the household of the Cherokee family and of one blood," and he urged them "to rekindle our social fire." But he also asserted that the new arrivals had "removed in their National Capacity and constitute a large majority," an indication that he expected their political institutions to prevail. Nevertheless, he proposed that representatives of the two groups enter into negotiations to find an equitable solution to the problem of government, for "a House divided against itself cannot stand."[7]

Ross insisted on the continuation of the eastern Cherokee government for several reasons. The Cherokee Nation, unlike the Old Settlers, had a written constitution and a far more elaborate law code and government, and they did constitute a substantial majority. In addition, he feared that the Old Settlers might accept the Treaty of New Echota in the name of the Nation and in violation of the Aquohee resolution. Ross did not want the Old Settlers in charge of the funds due the emigrants under the treaty, which were supposed to go for the cost of removal, claims for property destroyed or left in the East, and per capita payments. He also intended to try to renegotiate the treaty in order to secure additional funds. Finally, the Old Settlers had been entirely too welcoming to members of the Treaty Party who now sought to enhance their own political standing by hitching themselves to the Old Settlers. The United States saw the Treaty Party as true patriots, Ross as a villain, and the recent emigrants as guileless "savages." Consequently, when Major Ridge, John Ridge, Elias Boudinot, and Stand Watie showed up and began conferring with the Old Settler chiefs at Takatoka, Ross worried that they would influence the federal government to recognize the authority of the Old Settlers. The Old Settlers assured him that the eastern government could deal with all matters related to the treaty, an action that threatened to divide the Cherokees into two nations, but they also requested the Cherokee agent to pay the entire annuity, which previously had been divided, to them as the legitimate Cherokee government, a request that the agent declined until he received further instructions or the Cherokees resolved their political crisis.

On June 21 as the Takatoka council was breaking up, two contradictory courses emerged. Sequoyah, an Old Settler who had developed the syllabary for writing Cherokee, and Jesse Bushyhead, an eastern Cherokee Baptist minister who had

Sequoyah moved west of the Mississippi in 1818, perfected a system he invented for writing the Cherokee language in 1821, and worked to reunite the Nation after the removal of 1838–39. From Thomas L. McKenney and James Hall, History of the Indian Tribes of North America *(Philadelphia: F. W. Greenough, 1838–44); copy in the Rare Book Collections, Wilson Library, University of North Carolina, Chapel Hill.*

served as clerk to the council and headed a removal detachment, proposed a compromise. They suggested that the Cherokees meet on July 1 in a council at which the people could determine what kind of government they wanted. Those present agreed, although the plan clearly favored the far more numerous National Party, and the Takatoka council ended. Remaining behind were 100 to 150 National Party men who met secretly to decide what to do about the Treaty Party. John

Ross was not among them, but his son Allen was. In the view of these men, the Cherokees who had signed the Treaty of New Echota were traitors who had violated the Cherokee law prohibiting the unauthorized sale of land, and they drew up a list of those they believed should suffer the penalty prescribed by the law—death. Clan kin of the condemned men agreed, and parties formed to carry out the sentences.

We do not know exactly who the National Party men marked for execution, but three Cherokees paid with their lives for signing the treaty. Early on the morning of June 22, one group dragged John Ridge from his bed and, as his wife screamed, stabbed him to death. A little later, another party fired on Major Ridge as he traveled along a road in Washington County, Arkansas, killing him instantly. About the same time, a third group came to Elias Boudinot's house and asked him for some medicine, which was kept at the nearby mission. As he led them in that direction, they attacked him and split his head with a tomahawk. Missionary Samuel Austin Worcester, who lived nearby, sent word to Stand Watie, Boudinot's brother and fellow treaty signer, to flee, which he did. Distraught over the deaths of his brother, uncle, and cousin, Watie vowed revenge and started raising a company to kill John Ross. Mrs. Boudinot warned the chief that he should "leave home for safety," but Ross refused. "Why I am thus to be murdered without guilt of any crime," Ross wrote to the commander at Fort Gibson, "I cannot conceive."[8] Others recognized the danger the chief was in, however, and armed men surrounded his house.

Only about two thousand Cherokees met at the Illinois Camp Ground near Tahlequah on July 1. Most of those present were from the National Party, and they moved immediately to grant pardons to those accused of murdering members of the Treaty Party and to declare anyone who advocated revenge for the deaths of Boudinot and the Ridges an outlaw. The resolution offered amnesty to those involved if they apologized publicly within eight days, later extended, but denied them the right to hold office for five years. The council also established a police force to keep order. Then it moved to the business of governing.

On July 12, representatives of the few Old Settlers who attended the council and John Ross signed an act of union. They invited other Old Settlers to join them, and some did, but other Old Settlers and the Treaty Party remained opposed to any government dominated by the National Party. They held their own councils, and they sent delegates to Washington to seek federal protection and the arrest of the persons responsible for the deaths of Boudinot and the Ridges. Ignoring these other councils, the council at the Illinois Camp Ground forged ahead. On September 6, the council ratified a constitution very similar to the one that had organized Cherokee government in the East. They elected officers, one-third of whom were Old Settlers, John Ross became principal chief, and an Old Settler became second principal chief. Nevertheless, most Old Settlers continued to resist the act of union, and the Treaty Party bitterly opposed any concession to the National Party. Violence escalated and claimed, among others, the son of Sequoyah, who had tried to broker an agreement. Secretary of War Joel Poinsett, giving a sympathetic ear to the Treaty Party, insisted that Ross had illegally overthrown the legitimate government of the Old Settlers and demanded that he arrest the murderers of the Treaty Party leaders. He also refused payment of Cherokee annuities and funds due under the Treaty of New Echota to the Ross government.

Freezing Cherokee funds exacerbated the economic crisis in the Cherokee Nation. The Cherokee government depended on annuities for operating expenses, and Ross still owed contractors for expenses incurred during the removal. In order to function, the Cherokee Nation had to borrow money, and its national debt rose precipitously. Cherokee emigrants also desperately needed the money from spoliation claims and per capita payments due them under the Treaty of New Echota. Without these funds, they could not buy livestock, farm equipment, or even seeds. So they, too, resorted to credit, but the amount the poorest Cherokees, those most in need, could borrow was extremely limited. Consequently, a delegation from the National Party went to Washington to try to obtain the money due and, if possible, renegotiate the treaty to increase the amount the Cherokees received for their homeland. Ross also hoped to acquire a fee simple title for the lands in the West. With Democrat Martin Van Buren in the White House, he achieved little. While he was gone, however, the commanding officer at Fort Gibson, a federal fort in the Cherokee Nation, managed to broker a deal with the Old Settlers, who agreed to accept a revised act of union that promised them adequate representation and a share of the per capita payments. Some of these later repudiated the agreement, but it provided Ross with a firm basis for contending that his government was the legitimate government of the Nation.

In 1840 the Whigs won the presidency, and the next year Ross got a friendlier reception and payment of one hundred thousand dollars from the Cherokees' annuity fund, but he was not able to obtain a new treaty. Nor was he able to quiet federal insistence that he bring those responsible for the deaths of the Ridges and Boudinot to justice. Treaty Party members contended that their lives continued to be in jeopardy, took refuge in Arkansas, and appealed to the United States to protect them and their property. They found a surprisingly sympathetic ear in Washington, especially after the death of William Henry Harrison brought John Tyler to the presidency, and the new secretary of war held up payments for individual claims. As long as the National Party refused to accept the Treaty of New Echota, no per capita payments would be forthcoming, so Ross became the subject of growing criticism among Cherokees. Finally he secured payment of over a half million dollars for debts stemming from removal and paid off some of the Nation's creditors, but this did little to help people who desperately needed per capita payments.

In December 1841, Ethan Allen Hitchcock attended a meeting of the Cherokee council, which was trying to decide its course of action. Hitchcock was in Indian Territory investigating charges of corruption and fraud in the provisioning of southern Indians during and after their removal. The emigrant Cherokees had been in the West for over two years, but Hitchcock found many of them to be living in appalling conditions. Although some Cherokees had managed to build substantial log houses or buy them from Old Settlers, others lived in abject poverty. They had neither axes to fell trees for building shelters nor hoes to cultivate crops. One of the Cherokees he interviewed told him that "they were more comfortable East of the Mississippi, but that the mode of removal deprived great numbers of what little property, stock, etc., and that they had no means of supplying themselves here" because they "can neither get pay for their losses nor the per capita under the treaty of 1835." Perhaps most pitiful were the children who had lost their parents and had to depend "upon the charity of those who are frequently scarcely able to take care of themselves."[9] Yet Hitchcock remarked on the generosity of the well-to-do, who had livestock and foodstuff that they "shared among the poor with a kindliness and liberality that have not been learned from the whites."[10] He also marveled at the council's plan for the future, in particular its establishment of a public school system. Hitchcock formed a favorable opinion of the Cherokees, their government, and their principal chief, although he suspected that Ross was "ambitious of elevating his nation into perfect independence."[11]

In order to affirm the sovereignty of the Cherokee Nation and to alleviate the suffering of his people, Ross pressed for a renegotiation of the fraudulent Treaty of New Echota. The secretary of war flatly denied the possibility of a payment greater than $5 million. More alarmingly, he introduced the concept of allotting the commonly held Nation to individuals who would hold their land privately. Such action would encourage the influx of whites and the alienation of Cherokee land. Furthermore, it would destroy the Cherokee Nation, which would no longer have territory over which to exercise its sovereignty. The secretary did toss Ross one bone—he agreed to establish a commission to investigate spoliation claims of the Cherokees. Ross returned home and began documenting the claims, but the council was so discouraged that it declined to send a delegation to Washington in 1843.

While Ross was in Washington in the summer of 1842, violence in the Cherokee Nation escalated as members of the Treaty Party began killing individuals who they believed had been responsible for the deaths of their leaders. Individuals responsible for the trial, conviction, and punishment of Treaty Party members for other offenses also became targets. In August 1843 a group of armed men attacked officials counting ballots in the national election, which Ross won. They killed one of them, injured the other two, and destroyed the ballots. Gangs began to attack, rob, and kill other Cherokee citizens, most of whom were identified with the National Party, but it became impossible to distinguish between political violence and common crime. The Starr gang, for example, coalesced around James Starr, a signer of the

Treaty of New Echota. Under the guise of political resistance, Starr's sons and others terrorized the Cherokee Nation. In 1843, they murdered a white visitor to the Cherokee Nation as well as a white trader and his Cherokee wife, and burned the trader's house. Two years later, they burst into the home of John Ross's daughter, Jane Meigs, who happened to be away. They threatened two of her slaves, demanding to know their mistress's whereabouts, and then looted and torched the house. The slaves and Jane's husband managed to escape with their lives but little else. The Starr gang apparently had planned to rob and murder Lewis Ross's wealthy son-in-law as well. The Light Horse Guard had little success in bringing most perpetrators to justice, since their authority did not extend into Arkansas and Missouri where the outlaws fled. The violence gave the federal government an excuse to continue troops at Fort Gibson, decry the inefficacy of the Nation's government, and meddle further in Cherokee affairs. The Treaty Party and Old Settlers renewed their hope of undermining Ross's authority, since federal officials tended to blame Ross for the carnage.

In August 1844, in the midst of the chaos, a United States commission arrived to hear individual claims. Ross had been gathering information for two years and had compiled over four thousand claims worth more than $4 million. The commission promptly rejected many of the claims, virtually all of them from the National Party, since they occurred after May 23, 1838, the date by which the Cherokees were supposed to have vacated their homes in the East. A second group of federal officials arrived in November to investigate charges by the Treaty Party and Old Settlers that "grievous oppressions are practiced on them by the Ross or dominant party, insomuch that they cannot enjoy their liberty, property, and lives in safety; and that it was impossible for them to live in peace in the same community with their alleged oppressors."[12] The Old Settlers claimed that they had never agreed to the act of union and that the National Party forced them to live under its constitution and laws. Over the objections of Ross and the council, the commission met first with the Treaty Party and Old Settlers, then at Fort Gibson, and finally at the capital at Tahlequah. Many of the people at the hearings pressed for a division of the Nation. The situation at the end of 1844 looked gloomy indeed.

In January 1845, the commission made its report. Much to the surprise of everyone, the commissioners vindicated the National Party. Only 908 dissidents had turned out to meet with them, and of this number, 155 were white men. Most of these had but one complaint against the Cherokee government—they had not received their per capita payments. As for having the constitution foisted upon them, "The now complaining parties," the commissioners found, "acquiesced quietly in the new government" in an agreement negotiated at Fort Gibson in June 1840.[13] Furthermore, Old Settlers held offices in the new government and voted in its elections. The commission had minor reservations about the way the government had protected liberty and property, but in general supported its actions. As for being deprived of their liberty, the Light Horse had indeed arrested people, but they had done so "for the maintenance of peace and good order."[14] The charge that the government failed to protect their property came from the nationalization of salines, springs from which Cherokee entrepreneurs extracted salt, but even the Old Settlers' laws recognized that minerals like salt belonged to the Nation, and the Nation made fair valuations in order to reimburse owners for improvements. The commissioners denied that dissidents were in any particular danger, pointing to the widespread violence that claimed victims of all political persuasions, and attributed the lawlessness to "banditti." Urging the secretary of war to reject any effort to divide the Cherokee Nation, the commissioners indirectly criticized the long-standing practice of giving official hearing to dissident factions: "Nothing is more calculated to keep alive the flame of discord in the Cherokee nation, than the belief that the restless or discontented, though comparatively few in number, will always find a ready audience at Washington."[15] Finally, the commission recommended the negotiation of a new treaty. But further difficulties lay ahead.

The Democrats once again captured the White House, and James K. Polk took office in the spring of 1845. Polk had little sympathy for the Cherokees, and his secretary of war refused to accept Ross as the legitimate chief of the nation. Murders and robberies in the Cherokee Nation increased, and the council strengthened the Light Horse Guard. Stand Watie and his followers responded by fortifying an old army post, and other Treaty Party families fled to Arkansas where

United States citizens demanded protection from the United States Army. In the spring of 1846, the Old Settlers and the Treaty Party, along with the Cherokee Nation, sent delegates to Washington, but a resolution of the crisis seemed impossible. The president and Congress began to move toward a permanent division of the Cherokee Nation. In one final effort for unity, President Polk appointed a commission to try to hammer out a treaty. The result was the Treaty of 1846, to which all sides agreed "so that peace and harmony may be restored among them."[16]

The Treaty of 1846 contained a number of concessions that Ross had been forced to make. A general amnesty was extended to all citizens of the Cherokee Nation who had committed "offences and crimes." The signatories were grouped by faction, and some provisions applied only to one group or the other. The treaty awarded the Old Settlers per capita payments under the Treaty of New Echota and compensation from the Cherokee Nation for the salines it had seized. The Treaty Party benefited even more. The United States agreed to pay the Treaty Party one hundred thousand dollars for "losses and damages sustained by them" since removal and five thousand dollars each to the families of Major Ridge, John Ridge, and Elias Boudinot. The Cherokee Nation received compensation for the destruction of its printing press and other property. But the treaty also had provisions that united the body politic. It affirmed the title of all Cherokees to land in Arkansas and in the East, thereby denying the Old Settlers' claim to exclusive ownership of the western lands and assuring them of per capita payments for land ceded in the East. It guaranteed the Cherokees' title to their lands in the West, bound the parties to enact and enforce a code of laws "for the security of life, liberty, and property," and ensured trial by jury. The treaty also provided that claims already paid out of the $5 million the Cherokees had been awarded for their homeland would be restored to the fund, increasing the amount available for per capita distribution. The Senate ratified the treaty on August 7, 1846. Further negotiations followed, and the Old Settlers and North Carolina Cherokees, who also received compensation for the loss of their homeland, received payments in 1851. Final per capita payments were not made to the members of the Ross and Treaty parties until 1852. Each of these Cherokees received $92.79. Cherokees could now begin to be "settled," as both Meigs and Watie had wished.

The Treaty of 1846 brought a period of peace and stability to the Cherokee Nation. Even before the truce the Nation had established a public school system and begun publication of the *Cherokee Advocate,* a bilingual newspaper. In 1851 the Nation opened the Cherokee Male and Female Seminaries, or high schools. These pioneering institutions of public education began to provide bilingual Cherokee teachers for the public schools, which previously had depended heavily on white teachers. But financial problems continued to plague the Nation, and in 1856 the seminaries closed.

Political hostility, which smoldered during the years of apparent tranquility, erupted in 1861 when the Cherokee

Nation became embroiled in the Civil War. Ross favored neutrality; the Treaty Party openly sided with the Confederacy. Cherokee laws recognized and protected slavery, and many members of the political and economic elite were slaveholders, but the Cherokees also remembered who had dispossessed them. Initially forced into a treaty with the Confederacy, Ross fled the Nation in 1862 and took refuge behind Union lines. Following the war, he once again managed to thwart attempts to divide the Nation before he died in 1866.

Only after the Civil War did the factional scars of removal begin to heal, and Cherokee political parties developed along different lines. The Cherokees' Reconstruction Treaty, which reestablished relations with the United States, permitted the construction of railways across the Nation and opened the door to economic development, largely by non-Indians. By the 1880s, United States politicians and reformers alike were calling for the allotment of Cherokee land and the dissolution of tribal government. Compelled to enter into an agreement that accomplished these goals, the Cherokee Nation disappeared from maps when the Cherokees' western homeland became part of the state of Oklahoma in 1907. But Cherokees clung to John Ross's concept that their "National Capacity" transcended geographical boundaries. In 1976 the U.S. Supreme Court ruled that allotment agreements had not terminated tribal governments in Oklahoma. A new constitution, ratified in 1976 and revised in 2003, affirmed the sovereignty of the Cherokee Nation.

EPILOGUE

ON MAY 13, 2005, two Cherokee chiefs spoke at a ceremony in Chattanooga, Tennessee, that opened "The Passage," a pedestrian link between downtown and the Tennessee River. Chattanooga is built on land that once belonged to the Cherokees, and many of them embarked on the Trail of Tears from that very site. In his remarks, Principal Chief Michell Hicks of the Eastern Band of Cherokee Indians, who live in western North Carolina, reminded the audience about the "sorrowful" history that the Passage commemorates. "This is a Cherokee place," he said. "This place remembers before we were divided; when we were one great nation—the Cherokee Nation."[1] That division and the tragic journey known as the Trail of Tears took the ancestors of most Cherokees a thousand miles from Chattanooga and the Eastern Band to a new home in what is today Oklahoma. Chief Hicks pointed out the central role that that event continues to play in the identity of Cherokees today.

Principal Chief Chad Smith of the Cherokee Nation, whose citizens descend from those who were forced west, placed the Cherokees in a somewhat different context: "We are not a people of the past. We are a people of the present, and for many centuries, we will be a people of the future."[2] Even a tragedy as great as removal had not destroyed the Cherokees. Their continuing presence and the vitality of their culture were evident at this gathering. Five Cherokee artists from Oklahoma had created works for the Passage, and other Cherokees, including actor Wes Studi, were on hand for the ceremony.

The Cherokees intend to be around for a long time. Today there are 240,000 citizens of the Cherokee Nation and 10,000 members of the United Keetoowah Band in Oklahoma and 13,500 enrolled members of the Eastern Band in North Carolina. Thousands of other Americans have Cherokee ancestry. The Trail of Tears is their story, but it is also an American story. And if it is a story we are not proud of, we should make sure that its lesson is well learned: Racism, greed, and political partisanship can subvert even the noblest American ideals.

ACKNOWLEDGMENTS

THE AUTHORS ARE grateful to Colin Calloway of Dart-
mouth College and Carolyn Carlson of Viking/Penguin for
the invitation to write this little book. Principal Chief Chad
Smith of the Cherokee Nation, who developed a Cherokee
history course that is taught nationwide by Cherokee scholars, carefully read this manuscript and offered a number of
suggestions that we have incorporated. We appreciate his critique of this work and his deep and profound knowledge of
Cherokee history. We thank our graduate students at the
University of North Carolina, Rose Stremlau, Meg Devlin,
and Christina Snyder, for joining us in our enthusiasm for
Indian history and our conviction that writing about the past
really matters. We appreciate the time that Mary Young of
the University of Rochester took to read and critique the
manuscript. Mary knows more about Indian removal than
we ever will. Ray Fogelson of the University of Chicago had
no direct role in this book, but he had challenged us to think
about culture in much the same way that Mary had about
history. We have known them longer than we have known
each other, and our admiration of and affection for them is
reflected in the dedication.

NOTES

✹

INTRODUCTION

1. Sarah Vowell, "What I See When I Look at the Face on the $20 Bill," in *Take the Cannoli: Stories from the New World* (New York: Simon & Schuster, 2000), 157–58.

CHAPTER I

1. The standard source for the Cherokees' oral tradition is James Mooney, *Myths of the Cherokee* (Washington, D.C.: Bureau of American Ethnology, Nineteenth Annual Report, 1900). Mooney collected these stories among the Eastern Band in the late nineteenth century. A more recent collection is Barbara Duncan, *Living Stories of the Cherokees* (Chapel Hill: University of North Carolina Press, 1998). For Oklahoma folklore, see Jack F. and Anna G. Kilpatrick, *Friends of Thunder: Folktales of the Oklahoma Cherokees* (Dallas: Southern Methodist University Press, 1964).
2. Charles Hudson, *The Southeastern Indians* (Knoxville: University of Tennessee Press, 1976), especially Chapters 3 and 5, influenced the

discussion of the Cherokee belief system and the Cherokees' relationship to the land and its resources.

3. A superb guide to the Cherokee homeland is Barbara H. Duncan and Brett R. Riggs, *Cherokee Heritage Trails Guidebook* (Chapel Hill: University of North Carolina Press, 2003). For an imaginative exploration into the relationship of eastern Indians to the land, as well as other aspects of Native and European cultures, see Nancy Shoemaker, *A Strange Likeness: Becoming Red and White in Eighteenth-Century America* (New York: Oxford University Press, 2004).

4. James Mooney, *Sacred Formulas of the Cherokee* (Washington, D.C.: Bureau of American Ethnology, Seventh Annual Report, 1886), p. 342; Jack Frederick Kilpatrick and Anna Gritts Kilpatrick, *Walk in Your Soul: Love Incantations of the Oklahoma Cherokees* (Dallas: Southern Methodist University Press, 1965), 8.

5. Petition, June 30, 1818, Papers of the American Board of Commissioners for Foreign Missions, Houghton Library, Harvard University, Cambridge, Mass.

6. Gary C. Goodwin details the Cherokee ecosystem in *Cherokees in Transition: A Study of Changing Culture and Environment Prior to 1775* (Chicago: University of Chicago Department of Geography, Research Paper no. 181, 1977).

7. The standard archaeological studies of the Cherokees include Roy S. Dickens, *Cherokee Prehistory* (Knoxville: University of Tennessee Press, 1976), and Bennie C. Keel, *Cherokee Archaeology: A Study of the Appalachian Summit* (Knoxville: University of Tennessee Press, 1976). A more recent synthesis of research can be found in H. Trawick Ward and R. P. Stephen Davis, Jr., *Time Before History: The Archaeology of North Carolina* (Chapel Hill: University of North Carolina Press, 1999), Chapter 5.

8. Theda Perdue, *Cherokee Women: Gender and Culture Change, 1700–1835* (Lincoln: University of Nebraska Press, 1998), Chapters 1 and 2.

9. See Charles Hudson, *Knights of Spain, Warriors of the Sun: Hernando de Soto and the South's Ancient Chiefdoms* (Athens: University of Georgia Press, 1997), and *The Juan Pardo Expeditions: Exploration of the Carolinas*

and Tennessee, 1566–1568 (Washington: Smithsonian Institution Press, 1990).

10. Peter H. Wood, "The Changing Population of the Colonial South: An Overview by Race and Region, 1685–1790," *Powhatan's Mantle: Indians in the Colonial Southeast*, ed. Peter H. Wood, Gregory A. Waselkov, and M. Thomas Hatley (Lincoln: University of Nebraska Press, 1989), pp. 35–103.

11. John Philip Reid, *A Better Kind of Hatchet: Law, Trade, and Diplomacy in the Cherokee Nation During the Early Years of European Contact* (University Park: Pennsylvania State University Press, 1976).

12. Thomas Jefferson, *Notes on the State of Virginia* (original ed., 1785; Boston: Lilly and Wait, 1832), 302.

13. The best study of the Cherokees in the colonial period is Tom Hatley, *The Dividing Paths: Cherokees and South Carolinians Through the Era of Revolution* (New York: Oxford University Press, 1993).

14. Fred Gearing, *Priests and Warriors: Social Structures for Cherokee Politics in the 18th* Century (American Anthropological Association, Memoir 93, 1962), and V. Richard Persico, Jr., "Early Nineteenth-Century Political Organization," in *The Cherokee Indian Nation: A Troubled History*, ed. Duane H. King (Knoxville: University of Tennessee Press, 1979), 92–109.

15. Charles C. Royce, *The Cherokee Nation of Indians* (Washington, D.C.: Bureau of American Ethnology, 1887), chronicles land loss.

16. "Moore's Narrative," *North Carolina University Magazine*, 1888, quoted in James Mooney, *Myths*, 52–53.

CHAPTER 2

1. Sally M. Reese to Reverend Daniel Campbell, July 25, 1828, John Howard Payne Papers, Newberry Library, Chicago.

2. Henry Knox to George Washington, July 7, 1789, *American State Papers: Indian Affairs,* 1: 53.

3. Charles J. Kappler, comp. and ed., *Indian Affairs, Laws and Treaties* (Washington, D.C.: Government Printing Office, 1904), 2: 8–11 (Treaty of Hopewell), 2: 29–33 (Treaty of Holston).

4. Treaty of Holston, Kappler, *Laws and Treaties*, 2: 29–33.

5. Knox to Washington, July 7, 1789, *American State Papers: Indian Affairs,* 1: 53.

6. The most important works on the history of the Indian policy of the first decades of the United States remain Reginald Horsman, *Expansion and American Indian Policy, 1783–1812* (East Lansing: Michigan State University Press, 1967), and Francis Paul Prucha, *American Indian Policy in the Formative Years: The Indian Trade and Intercourse Acts, 1790–1834* (Cambridge: Harvard University Press, 1962).

7. For missionaries among the Cherokees, see William G. McLoughlin, *Cherokees and Missionaries, 1789–1839* (New Haven: Yale University Press, 1984).

8. For the newspaper, see Theda Perdue, ed., *Cherokee Editor: The Writings of Elias Boudinot* (Knoxville: University of Tennessee Press, 1983), 85–154.

9. Theda Perdue, *Slavery and the Evolution of Cherokee Society, 1540–1866* (Knoxville: University of Tennessee Press, 1979), Chapter 4.

10. Perdue, *Cherokee Women,* Chapter 5.

11. Meigs to Dearborn, June 11, 1808, Records of the Cherokee Agency in Tennessee, 1801–1835, U.S. Bureau of Indian Affairs, Record Group 75, National Archives, Washington, D.C., Microcopy M-208.

12. For Cherokee political history between the American Revolution and removal, see William G. McLoughlin, *Cherokee Renascence in the New Republic* (Princeton: Princeton University Press, 1986).

13. Council at Ustanali to Meigs, April 11, 1810, M-208.

14. *Laws of the Cherokee Nation: Adopted by the Council at Various Periods* (Tahlequah, C.N.: Cherokee Advocate Office, 1852), 4–5.

15. *Laws,* 45.

16. *Laws,* 118.

CHAPTER 3

1. *Cherokee Phoenix,* November 12, 1831.

2. Joseph McMinn to William H. Crawford, October 25, 1816, *American State Papers: Indian Affairs,* 2: 115.

3. George M. Troup to John C. Calhoun, February 28, 1824, *American State Papers: Indian Affairs,* 2: 475–76.

4. Quoted in McLoughlin, *Cherokee Renascence,* 302.

5. *Christian Herald,* December 20, 1823; quoted in Thurman Wilkins, *Cherokee Tragedy: The Story of the Ridge Family and of the Decimation of a People* (New York: Macmillan, 1970), 145.

6. *American Eagle,* March 22, 1824; quoted in Wilkins, 148.

7. *Niles Register,* July 9, 1825; quoted in Wilkins, 150.

8. This history is best covered in Wilkins, Chapter 6, and in Ralph Gabriel, *Elias Boudinot, Cherokee, and His America* (Norman: University of Oklahoma Press, 1941).

9. *Cherokee Phoenix,* November 12, 1831.

10. John C. Calhoun to the House of Representatives, December 5, 1818, *American State Papers: Indian Affairs,* 2: 183.

11. Andrew Jackson to President James Monroe, March 4, 1817, in John S. Bassett, ed., *Correspondence of Andrew Jackson* (Washington, D.C.: Carnegie Institute, 1926–35), 2: 277–82.

12. Return J. Meigs to William Eustis, April 5, 1811; quoted in McLoughlin, *Renascence,* 165–66.

13. Return J. Meigs to John C. Calhoun, November 22, 1822; quoted in McLoughlin, *Renascence,* 303.

14. John Ross and Cherokee Delegation to John C. Calhoun, January 19, 1824; quoted in McLoughlin, *Renascence,* 307.

15. Articles of Agreement, April 24, 1802, *American State Papers: Public Lands,* 1: 114.

16. President James Monroe to the Senate and House of Representatives of the United States, in James D. Richardson, comp., *The Messages and Papers of the Presidents* (New York: Bureau of National Literature, 1897), 2: 803–05.

17. *Acts of the Georgia General Assembly,* 1827, 1: 249.

18. *Acts of the Georgia General Assembly,* 1828, 1: 88–89.

19. Andrew Jackson, First Annual Message, December 8, 1829, in Richardson, *Messages,* 3: 1019–22.

20. Jeremiah Evarts, *Cherokee Removal: The "William Penn" Essays and*

Other Writings, ed. Francis Paul Prucha (Knoxville: University of Tennessee Press, 1981).

21. Mary Hershberger, "Mobilizing Women, Anticipating Abolition: The Struggle against Indian Removal in the 1830s," *Journal of American History* 86 (1999): 15–40.

22. *Debates in Congress*, Twenty-first Congress, first session, 325, 328; quoted in Ronald N. Satz, *American Indian Policy in the Jacksonian Era* (Lincoln: University of Nebraska Press, 1975), 24.

23. *United States Statutes at Large*, 4: 411–12.

24. Martin Van Buren, *Autobiography*, ed. John C. Fitzpatrick, *Annual Report*, American Historical Association, 1918, 2: 274–96.

CHAPTER 4

1. John Ross to Jeremiah Evarts, July 24, 1830, Gary Moulton, ed., *The Papers of Chief John Ross* (2 v., Norman: University of Oklahoma Press, 1985), 1: 195–96.

2. The major work on John Ross, the central figure in this chapter, is Gary Moulton, *John Ross, Cherokee Chief* (Athens: University of Georgia Press, 1978). An important and recent assessment is Mary Young, "John Ross: Cherokee Chief and Defender of the Nation," in Michael A. Morrison, ed., *The Human Tradition in Antebellum America* (Wilmington: Scholarly Resources, 2000), 115–30. The fullest discussion of Ross's political strategy during the removal crisis is Walter H. Conser, Jr., "John Ross and the Cherokee Resistance Campaign," *Journal of Southern History*, 44 (May 1978), 191–212.

3. Hugh Montgomery to George Gilmer, July 2, 1831, Document TCC525, Southeastern Native American Documents, 1730–1842, Galileo Digital Library of Georgia Database, http://io.gsu.edu/cgi-bin/homepage.cgi.

4. Hugh Montgomery to John Eaton, February 18, 1830, Certificate of Abraham Birdwell, February 9, 1830, James W. Williams to Montgomery, March 4, 1830, House Executive Document 89, Twenty-first Congress, first session, Serial 197, 30–31, 37–38.

5. John Ross, "To the Cherokee People," April 14, 1831, Moulton, ed., *Ross Papers*, 1: 217.

6. *Cherokee Phoenix*, January 8, 1831.
7. *The Cherokee Nation* v. *The State of Georgia,* January Term, 1831, 5 Peters 1-80. Marshall's opinion is at 14-20. The argument of Wirt and Sergeant is at 2-11, the dissenting opinions are at 20-79.
8. Ross, "To the Cherokee People," April 14, 1831, Moulton, ed., *Ross Papers*, 1: 215–19.
9. *Cherokee Phoenix,* April 9, 1831.
10. *Samuel A. Worcester* v. *The State of Georgia,* January Term, 1832, 6 Peters 562.
11. Ibid., 536–61.
12. Tim Alan Garrison, *The Legal Ideology of Removal: The Southern Judiciary and the Sovereignty of Native American Nations* (Athens: University of Georgia Press, 2002), and Jill Norgren, *The Cherokee Cases: The Confrontation of Law and Politics* (New York: McGraw-Hill, 1996), are important recent interpretations of the Cherokee cases.
13. William W. Williamson to Wilson Lumpkin, April 28, 1832, Document TCC537, Southeastern Native American Documents, 1730–1842, Galileo Digital Library of Georgia Database.

CHAPTER 5

1. Elias Boudinot, "Letters and Other Papers Relating to Cherokee Affairs: Being a Reply to Sundry Publications Authorized by John Ross," in Theda Perdue, ed., *Cherokee Editor: The Writings of Elias Boudinot* (Knoxville: University of Tennessee Press, 1983), 162.
2. In addition to the sources cited, this chapter relies on Moulton, *John Ross*; Wilkins, *Cherokee Tragedy*; and Wilson Lumpkin, *The Removal of the Cherokee Indians from Georgia, 1827–1841* (New York: Dodd, Mead, 1907).
3. John Ridge to Stand Watie, April 6, 1832, in Edward Everett Dale and Gaston Litton, eds., *Cherokee Cavaliers: Forty Years of Cherokee History as Told in the Correspondence of the Ridge-Watie-Boudinot Family* (Norman: University of Oklahoma Press, 1939), 7–10.
4. Ibid.
5. Bassett, 4: 430; S. C. Stambaugh and Amos Kendall to William L. Marcy, December 26, 1845, "Cherokee disturbances. Message from the

President of the United States, relative to the Cherokee difficulties," H. doc. 185, Twenty-ninth Congress, first session, Serial 485, 50.

6. Ridge to Ross, February 2, 1833, in Moulton, *Ross Papers*, 1: 259–60.

7. Ross, Annual Message, October 15, 1833, in Moulton, *Ross Papers*, 1: 270.

8. Ross et al. to Andrew Jackson, March 12, 1834, in Moulton, *Ross Papers*, 1: 279.

9. Wilkins, 251–52.

10. Wilson Lumpkin to John Forsyth, May 30, 1834, in Lumpkin, 1: 262.

11. "Gold Rush," *New Georgia Encyclopedia*, http://www.georgiaencyclopedia.org/nge/Article.jsp?id=h-785.

12. Lumpkin to Jackson, May 20, 1835, in Lumpkin, 1: 348.

13. Ridge to Ross, December 4, 1835, in Moulton, *Ross Papers*, 1: 377.

14. Lumpkin to William Bishop, August 16, 1835, in Lumpkin, 1: 360–61; Lumpkin, Annual Message, November 3, 1835, in Lumpkin, 1: 166.

15. *Acts of the Georgia General Assembly*, 1835, 1: 105–7.

16. Treaty with the Cherokee, 1835, in Kappler, 2: 439–49.

17. William Schley to Jackson, February 13, 1836, Georgia Governor's Letter Book, in "Early State Records," *Records of the States of the United States of America* (Washington, D.C.: Library of Congress, 1949–51), E.2, Reel 4, Unit 1.

CHAPTER 6

1. William Shorey Coodey to John Howard Payne, August 13, 1840, John Howard Payne Papers, Newberry Library, Chicago, Ill.

2. The standard work that chronicles the removal of the southeastern Indians is Grant Foreman, *Indian Removal: The Emigration of the Five Civilized Tribes of Indians* (Norman: University of Oklahoma Press, 1932). This chronology relies on Foreman. Two collections of primary documents are Theda Perdue and Michael D. Green, eds., *The Cherokee Removal: A Brief History with Documents* (2nd ed., Boston: Bedford/St. Martin's, 2005), and Vicki Rozema, ed., *Voices from the Trail of Tears* (Winston-Salem, N.C.: John F. Blair, 2003). The entire third (summer) issue of *Journal of Cherokee Studies* 3 (1978) is devoted to documents from removal. For an anthology of insightful articles, see William

L. Anderson, ed., *Cherokee Removal: Before and After* (Athens: University of Georgia Press, 1991).

3. Treaty with the Western Cherokees, 1828, Article 8, Kappler, 2: 290.

4. These figures come from Jack D. Baker's transcription, *Cherokee Emigration Rolls, 1817–1835* (Oklahoma City: Baker Publishing Co., 1977).

5. Foreman, 252–63.

6. Brigadier General John E. Wool to the Cherokees, March 22, 1837, Rozema, 69.

7. H. G. Clauder to Theodore Schultz, March 17, 1837; quoted in Wilkins, 290.

8. B. B. Cannon's Journal, in Rozema, 90.

9. Sarah H. Hill, "Cherokee Removal: Forts Along the Georgia Trail of Tears" (The National Park Service and the Georgia Department of Natural Resources/Historic Preservation Division, March 2005, http://www.nps.gov/trte/TRTE/Georgias%20Trail%20of%20Tears%20Report%20ONLY.pdf).

10. Foreman, 302–3.

11. Daniel S. Butrick, *The Journal of Rev. Daniel S. Butrick, May 19, 1838–April 1, 1839* (Park Hill, Okla.: Trail of Tears Association, Oklahoma Chapter, 1998), 2, 8.

12. Butrick, 6.

13. John Finger, *The Eastern Band of Cherokees, 1819–1900* (Knoxville: University of Tennessee Press, 1984), 20–40.

14. Butrick, 10.

15. Ibid., 7.

16. *Missionary Herald* 34 (1838); quoted in Foreman, 296.

17. Petition, June 11, 1838, M-208.

18. Butrick, 32.

19. Nat Smith to J. W. Harris, July 3, 1838; quoted in Foreman, 298.

20. Butrick, 32.

21. Winfield Scott to J. Ross, E. Hicks, J. Brown, and others, August 1, 1838, in Emmet Starr, *History of the Cherokee Indians and their Legends and Folk Lore* (orig. ed. 1921; Muskogee, Okla.: Hoffman Printing Co., 1984), 100–101. The ultimate cost of removal, which took longer and required far more supplies than anyone anticipated, was $1,263,338.38.

22. Winfield Scott to John Ross, Elijah Hicks, James Brown, Edward Gunter, Situwakee, White Path, and Richard Taylor, August 22, 1838, Moulton, *Ross Papers*, 1: 659–62.

23. J. Ross, R. Taylor, J. Brown, E. Hicks, and White Path to Winfield Scott, August 25, 1838, Moulton, *Ross Papers*, 1: 662–65.

24. John Benge, George C. Lowry, and George Lowrey to John Ross, September 29, 1838, Moulton, *Ross Papers*, 1: 673–74.

25. This information comes from *Trail of Tears National Historic Trail: Comprehensive Management and Use Plan* (U.S. Department of the Interior, National Park Service, Denver Service Center, 1992).

26. Finger, 20–40.

27. George Hicks to John Ross, November 4, 1838, Moulton, *Ross Papers*, 1: 687.

28. *New York Observer*, January 26, 1839, quoted in Foreman, 305–7.

29. Butrick, 55.

30. Jesse Bushyhead to John Ross, October 21, 1838, Moulton, *Ross Papers*, 1: 683.

31. *New York Observer*, January 26, 1839, quoted in Foreman, 305–7.

32. Interview of Rachel Dodge in the Indian Pioneer papers, Oklahoma Historical Society, quoted in Carolyn Ross Johnston, *Cherokee Women in Crisis: Trail of Tears, Civil War, and Allotment, 1838–1907* (Tuscaloosa: University of Alabama Press, 2003), 73.

33. *New York Observer*, January 26, 1839, quoted in Foreman, 305–7.

34. Foreman, 302–3.

35. Butrick, 48.

36. Russell Thornton, "The Demography of the Trail of Tears Period: A New Estimate of Cherokee Population Losses," in Anderson, 75–95.

CHAPTER 7

1. Meigs to Ross, November 5, 1845, Moulton, *Ross Papers*, 2: 273–74.

2. Sarah Watie to Stand Watie, July 19, 1846, Dale and Litton, 45–46.

3. Benjamin F. Thompson deposition, January 12, 1842, "Right of President to Withhold Papers—Frauds on Indians. Message from the Presi-

dent of the United States, Transmitting the Report of Lieutenant Colonel Hitchcock, Respecting the Affairs of the Cherokee Indians, &c.," H. Doc. 219, Twenty-seventh Congress, third session, Serial 425, 82–83.

4. Ibid.

5. This narrative relies heavily on William G. McLoughlin, *After the Trail of Tears: The Cherokees' Struggle for Sovereignty* (Chapel Hill: University of North Carolina Press, 1993).

6. Resolution, August 1, 1838, Starr, 104–6.

7. Ross, "Address to a General Council of the Cherokees," June 10, 1839, Moulton, *Ross Papers*, 1: 712–13.

8. Ross to Matthew Arbuckle, Moulton, *Ross Papers*, June 22, 1839.

9. Ethan Allen Hitchcock, *A Traveler in Indian Territory: The Journal of Ethan Allen Hitchcock*, ed. Grant Foreman (original ed., 1930; reprint, Norman: University of Oklahoma Press, 1996), 54.

10. E. A. Hitchcock to J. C. Spencer, December 2, 1841, "Right of President," H. Doc. 219, Twenty-seventh Congress, third session, 7.

11. Hitchcock, *A Traveler,* 27.

12. William Wilkins to Commissioners, October 18, 1844, "Report of the Secretary of War, Communicating (in Compliance with a Resolution of the Senate) the Report and Correspondence of the Board of Inquiry, to Prosecute an Examination into the Causes and Extent of the Discontents and Difficulties among the Cherokee Indians," S. Doc. 140, Twenty-eighth Congress, second session, 2, Serial 457, 2.

13. Ibid., 7.

14. Ibid., 9.

15. Ibid., 11.

16. Kappler, 2: 561–65.

EPILOGUE

1. *Cherokee One Feather,* May 18, 2005.

2. Ibid.

SELECT BIBLIOGRAPHY

Anderson, William L., ed. *Cherokee Removal: Before and After.* Athens: University of Georgia Press, 1991.

Andrew, John A., III. *From Revivals to Removal: Jeremiah Evarts, the Cherokee Nation, and the Search for the Soul of America.* Athens: University of Georgia Press, 1992.

Conser, Walter H., Jr. "John Ross and the Cherokee Resistance Campaign, 1833–1838." *Journal of Southern History,* 44 (May 1978), 189–212.

Foreman, Grant. *Indian Removal: The Emigration of the Five Civilized Tribes of Indians.* Norman: University of Oklahoma Press, 1932.

Garrison, Tim Alan. *The Legal Ideology of Removal: The Southern Judiciary and the Sovereignty of Native American Nations.* Athens: University of Georgia Press, 2002.

Horsman, Reginald. *Expansion and American Indian Policy, 1783–1812.* East Lansing: Michigan State University Press, 1967.

McLoughlin, William G. *Cherokee Renascence in the New Republic.* Princeton: Princeton University Press, 1986.

———. *Cherokees and Missionaries, 1789–1839.* New Haven: Yale University Press, 1984.

Moulton, Gary E. *John Ross, Cherokee Chief.* Athens: University of Georgia Press, 1978.

Perdue, Theda, ed. *Cherokee Editor: The Writings of Elias Boudinot.* Knoxville: University of Tennessee Press, 1983.

Perdue, Theda. *Cherokee Women: Gender and Culture Change, 1700–1835.* Lincoln: University of Nebraska Press, 1998.

Perdue, Theda, and Michael D. Green, eds. *The Cherokee Removal: A Brief History with Documents.* Second edition. Boston: Bedford/St. Martin's, 2005.

Prucha, Francis Paul. *American Indian Policy in the Formative Years: The Indian Trade and Intercourse Acts, 1790–1834.* Cambridge: Harvard University Press, 1962.

Royce, Charles C. *The Cherokee Nation of Indians.* Fifth Annual Report, Bureau of American Ethnology, 1883–84. Washington, D.C.: Government Printing Office, 1887.

Rozema, Vicki. *Voices from the Trail of Tears.* Winston-Salem, N.C.: John F. Blair, 2003.

Satz, Ronald N. *American Indian Policy in the Jacksonian Era.* Lincoln: University of Nebraska Press, 1975.

Wallace, Anthony F. C. *The Long, Bitter Trail: Andrew Jackson and the Indians.* New York: Hill and Wang, 1993.

Watson, Harry L. *Liberty and Power: The Politics of Jacksonian America.* New York: Noonday Press, 1990.

Wilkins, Thurman. *Cherokee Tragedy: The Story of the Ridge Family and of the Decimation of a People.* New York: Macmillan, 1970.

Young, Mary E. "The Cherokee Nation: Mirror of the Republic." *American Quarterly,* 33 (1981), 502–24.

———."Conflict Resolution on the Indian Frontier." *Journal of the Early Republic,* 16 (1996), 1–19.

———."The Exercise of Sovereignty in Cherokee Georgia." *Journal of the Early Republic* 10 (1990): 43–63.

INDEX